How to Have Fun with Retirement

The lighter side of retired life

Patrick M. Kennedy

How to Have Fun with Retirement

ISBN: 978-1-60145-469-0

Printed in the United States of America

For Andy, Becky, Buzz, Babe, Deb, Diane, Don M, Don E, Drake, James, Jim, George, Patty, Ruth, Tina, Tom, Tommy, Sam, and Uncle Roy

This book is dedicated to all those who have already read the joke and turned the page.

Acknowledgments

I'd like to thank Allison St. Clair, Publisher of the Senior Wire News Service, for all of her encouragement while writing these articles. I also thank the people at Writers Press and Artist-Writers-Publishing for their assistance and help in getting this book published.

Table of Contents

Pre-Ramble

A while back I plunged into an unfamiliar environment when I decided to quit working and retire. Well, anyway, semi-retire. Not completely like the Airmail stamp or the 45 rpm record. I continue to poke my computer to life every morning with the hope of arousing the proper Muse to guide my pen (key strokes) through heavenly enlightenment and onward to the rock-solid ground, flight-of-the-imagination, land of Disney-type retirement.

Who am I? I figure I qualify as a fully experienced worker re-assigning my objectives toward the softer side of life. I have worked at a yellow-pages number of enlightening jobs in my personal history. Over time, I've labored as a paperboy, professional musician, elevator operator, shipping clerk, soldier, teletype operator, bartender, bar owner, janitor, graphic artist, advertising consultant, publisher, copywriter, art gallery owner, picture framer, salesman, a technical writer, poet, story teller and novelist, and a few occupations off the record I won't bring up.

I've seen all the sides and felt all the emotions of the work world. I have a living and breathing cluster of friends who are in or near retirement. This, I believe, provides me with a wide-ranging record of experience to call upon in my examination and communication about retirement fun. I have the solid qualifications to explore and write about what I should expect, and demand, in my coming years. On these pages I hope to somehow pass this information on to you.

Many of the essays and articles in this book have been published through the Senior Wire News Service, other periodicals and newspapers and on-line e-magazines, and some have become parts of published books. Some of the information here has been extracted from other sources and writers and retirees who have contributed to the pot.

Some of the opening questions I asked myself were, "Now that I have the time, what do I do with it?" and "Where do I do it?" and "How do I have fun with retirement?" and "With who?" And more importantly, "What is Fun in the first place?"

It was one of those light-bulb moments in life as rare as an ugly unicorn in Utah. Why not write about it ... and here I am.

One of the other questions, after those above, that crept from my fingertips, through my mind, and onto the PC monitor was, "What is retirement and how did I get into this conundrum of believing that I must retire in the first place"?

My research mode kicked in and I discovered, while enjoying a short hop through history, it was another thing I could blame on the Industrial Revolution.

For the greater part in early American history, people lived and worked on farms with extended families. In time, some of these Americans moved from farms and small rural communities to larger cities. In 1890, 28 % of the U.S. population lived in cities.

Then the gagging Industrial Revolution happened to us and spawned pollution and strings of production lines across the world. By 1930 this percentage had doubled to 56 %. People were working for other people and hourly wages, and not tilling the land for crops. Thus, industrial production took over the agricultural production society. So again, things did change.

The world's initial Social Security retirement program was put into effect, not in America, but in Germany in 1889, designed by Germany's legendary Chancellor, Otto von Bismarck, of sink-the-battleship fame. The copycat Americans, after the 30's Depression, enacted the Social Security Act and President Roosevelt signed it into law and created a new social attitude on August 14, 1935.

From that time on RETIREMENT became a part of the American language and a lifetime goal and dream for most: Free time to do what **I** want to do, at last.

You now, or will soon have, that same option.

And here we are. And here I am. Now what?

You see, my writing this book, and randomly dropping in some sorta-art, is my answer and solution and a personal response to the question:

How to Have Fun with Retirement?

∞ ∞ ∞ ∞ *Time without end to all* ∞ ∞ ∞ ∞

Introduction to This Fun

How to have fun with retirement? First, read this book, which is overloaded with absurdity as well as helpful information, while sitting under a tree or on the bank of a whispering flow of water. If you don't have a nearby creek or tree, turn on the faucet in your kitchen sink and sit next to the avocado plant or cactus scrub.

By definition, *fun* is a time or feeling of enjoyment or amusement, and r*etirement* is the status of a worker who has stopped working. These two definitions go in concert like popcorn and butter. In other and simpler terms, retirement must be like buying admission to tour an amusement park, and not paying the toll to travel on another expressway. The opposite of work has always been fun. Fun also is known by several aliases, such as enjoyment, pleasure, joy, entertainment, merriment, and it is absolutely the opposite of boredom.

It is quite a transitional shock to wake up that first Monday morning and realize you did not bounce out of bed, shoved out by the shrieking scream or disc-jockey chatter from your alarm clock, and you realize you can ecstatically flip it into the trashcan if you wish.

Life has changed, and so must you. There are so many alternatives and choices. You have thought them out and through and inside out & round about ... you are sure you have, but when that first glorious day off comes, that first Monday not at work, and especially the Tuesday, Wednesday and Thursday that follow, your new life style starts to hit the panic button --

"This is it" This is the first week of a new venture into all those promises of free time, FREE TIME, and all the guarantees of bliss and tranquility that go with it. Life will be good. Life will be fun. Life will be all fun and games from here on out:

Nothing but entertaining activities and Clarabell the Clown smiles from now on.

Soon, though, reality will appear to hit you in the face like a shot from Clarabell's squirt gun. Now what, you ask? You will begin to feel that today looks just like yesterday, and like all the others did last week. Free time has become Freeze Time. You find everyday functions; the trials and irritations as you knew them, being replaced by new everyday trials and irritations. *"That's life"*, you may say to yourself and completely accept it as the natural flow of things.

Not!

Looking backward through the reverse crystal ball, if your work days were 8-hours long and spaced around a 30 minute lunch and two 15 minute coffee breaks, odds are you didn't like going to work in the first place and you'll only miss the lunch and coffee breaks. If this is the case, you may be more prone to fall into the humdrum of a boring routine.

Don't Do It!

One solution is to imagine every half hour is a lunch break and you must cram as much fun and relaxation into it as you can. You did it for years each day at work, and you can do it again.

If your work days were any hours you wanted to work, or pretended to work, wrapped around a 3-martini lunch, it will be harder because you probably enjoyed your job and will really, really miss the lunches. The martinis should not be the focus from here on, although not completely omitted from the equation, but the '*pretending to work*' is the key. If you can pretend to work for money, you can pretend to '*live for fun*'. It's an easy transition.

A key in all cases is to develop the correct attitude through this transition and not allow boredom be the dominating emotion. Boredom can be infectious and cause the mind and body to shut down. One corny approach is to paste a note on your bathroom mirror that reads, "*Have Fun Today*".

Lets' face it; most of us, when we retire, *do not* have the option of becoming members of the Jet Set. We maintain our relatively comfortable and familiar prone position in the La-Z-Boy Recliner Set ... and therein lay the problem. The recliner is not a first-class seat aboard a plane that takes you somewhere. In order to get somewhere from a recliner, you must first get out of it.

Keep active: Stretch your brain. Not by watching more TV or reading the newspaper. Activate the brain by exposing yourself to things that are not so easy, such as new experiences. Shake up your daily routine, take day trips, go back to school or take classes, work the crossword puzzle every day, learn a new language, or just get a stimulating hobby: Go fishing. Learn to golf. Take up dancing. Buy an RV and travel. This all sounds easy to say, but doing is the fun part, not the hard part.

Turn that frown upside down.

There are dozens, if not gazillions, of books and magazine articles trying to simplify and clarify financial security, health and diet, insurance, and all the why-in-the-world-do-we-need-all-these-items-for-comfort books. They are important, of course. If you want to have fun, you must still be semi-rational, semi-sane, healthy as possible, and reasonably comfortable.

However, the social, physical and mind-set dispositions of retirement are just as important, if not more so than the mind-numbing subjects dollar-sign information dispenses. Money, or a Visa Card for that matter, does not buy happiness, although it makes it a great deal easier to jump over the tollgate from the work world to the land of leisure. Laughter buys happiness. Happiness should control your environment with a smile and a laugh; something for which you should strive.

It is the plan in these pages to address many aspects of the leisure world and their intrinsic problems with a lighthearted eye: Keep on smiling, keep on laughing and having fun, and create an upbeat attitude.

Murphy's Law *(If anything can go wrong, it will)* is a well-documented saw and possibly a proven philosophy by some comedic academic somewhere, sometime. However, here we discuss an optimistic approach to retirement. If things go wrong, and they will, no doubt about that, then just laugh it off and move on, because breaking Murphy's Law is not a penal offense ... there is no jail time.

How Mark Twain put it: "*The first half of life consists of the capacity to enjoy without the chance; the last half consists of the chance without the capacity."* This doesn't have to be the retirement philosophy in the modern age. You are healthier than Twain's generation and can live longer. Retirement, these days, isn't an automatic and robotic switch that clicks *ON* at a certain age. It is not even a certainty or even a line crossed into the next phase of life. Retirement in this generation of Boomers is an attitude rather than a chronological age. Groucho Marx, the comedian said, *"Getting older is no problem. You just have to live longer"*. These days, you just have to deal with it.

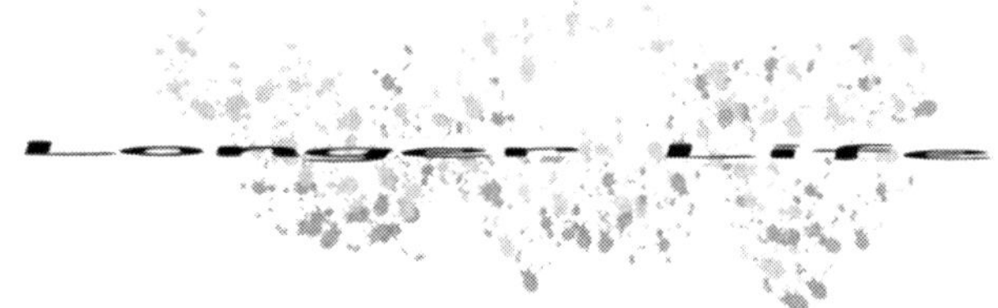

For starters, let's stop complaining about getting old. Stop obsessing about flaws. Who are you? What do you think you look like? What do you really look like? Who can answer these questions and be correct ... and even with a straight face? As the fist-fighting, spinach-loving sailor of comics and cartoons Popeye the Sailor said, *"I y'am what I y'am"*. For a cartoon character, he had a firm grasp and positive attitude. In addition, when it comes to a less-than-positive attitude toward life, another of his famous, spinach-induced sayings will help: *"That's all I can stands, I can't stands no more!"* The most important question you can ask is, "Who do I want to be?"

It is probably best to begin with a few upbeat facts and demands that are widely known, often not recognized, and sometimes completely avoided: Everyone can stand to lose 20 or 30 pounds, well lose it. There probably is one thing you always wanted to do, but never had the time or guts, well, do it. You cannot stand the exasperating rain, snow and cold beating on your body anymore, so move into the sun. You are bored with the idle time, so get a hobby or a dog, or heaven forbid, another job.

There are so many options: There is the significant and exciting option to join the giggles and warm-fuzzy feeling in the world of fun and play. Again, fun is a time or feeling of enjoyment or amusement; and there is always the part-time job option on the other hand, which is a regular activity performed in exchange for payment to augment the fun in life. This is sort of the antithesis of retirement, but sometimes unavoidable in these uneasy financial times. We have to be realistic as well as a soul-searching humanoid.

Fun? ... Work? ... Fun? ... Work? ... Such a tricky choice: There must be a life-threatening catch to this fun stuff vs. work stuff?

Not all of us want to dive into a new profession and call it RETIREMENT ... some do. In addition, most of us definitely don't want to become a reconfigured clone of that person we were who periodically picked up a paycheck and deposited it in a revolving-door bank account. Some of us actually have the aspiration to catch up with the world we missed while sleeping through work, and avoid falling back to the same-ol' routine of 9 to 5, and the *I think I'm still alive because I can hear the traffic going past me* way of life. If you want to be a retired and also be the perfect clone of the historical you, then save your genes in the fridge and come back in a hundred years and mate with a model: Move on to fun.

Again, looking backwards through that reverse crystal ball, there appears to be another way to approach the retirement years ahead. If you anticipate about 20 to 30 more years ahead of you to play and have fun, than ask yourself,

'What was I doing 20 or 30 years ago, and what have I accomplished in those years.'

Most will respond to themselves while looking in the mirror and brushing their teeth, *'I did this, I did that, I went here, and there, I met this person and got married, I met this person and had an affair, I started a business and failed at business, I had these jobs, I moved there, then there, I went to the World Series, I didn't parachute out of an airplane, I learned how to mambo and play a decent game of pool, I once believed Karaoke was a religion, and I can drink with the best of them.*

Which of these periods in your life was the most fun?

Of course, you can't leave all your experiences and talents and faults behind. You can't entirely build a new you. Some things you have to drag into the future with you. But you can take the better pieces of a scrambled background and fabricate a future based on them.

Try not being a copycat. Just because Duane down the road bought a 35-foot RV he uses two weeks out of the year, doesn't mean you have to. Maybe you can buy one and use it half the year, or all year, or never, who knows? Maybe you can convert it into a spare bedroom for guests or a wayward brother.

Just because Lilly from the local Muddy's Lounge and Grill created a garden of prize-winning, multi-colored, weedless plant life doesn't require you to take up the challenge. Maybe for you a simple avocado plant on the windowsill surrounded by ivy climbing around your collection of exotic beer bottles is good enough.

In these pages we will try to touch on some of retirement's Slice-of-Life experiences. These are brief encounters and happenstance familiarity with those itchy little things that will bug you, but are necessary, and sometimes unavoidable. They will include excellent and sometimes shocking aspects of our leisure time and decisions.

Also included are test questions only the experienced senior can answer; pet peeves; hints about travel, activities, and saving money; vital statistics that probably won't change anything, but are good to know. Throughout the book will be quotes from seniors from throughout the globe who have experienced the passage into retirement and are enjoying the ride.

And yes, a few jokes, fantasies and facts that are circling the Internet planet about old age and retirement, and there are many and they are funny.

Test Questions and Quotes:

Throughout this book will be questions to test your eligibility to claim you are really a full-grown, fully developed, and full-sized grown-up person on or near the retired Boomer's world. Following is an example.

The answers to the test questions are at the end of the book.

? What are Ricky's father, mother and brother's names?

Quotes from those seniors already having fun that have been collected from throughout the world.

"Having no real set schedule to follow unless I make it ...often, I have leisure days and nights." ...

Greg, Downsville, Louisiana

Quotes borrowed from people who have been there at different times and from different backgrounds.

"Humor is reason gone mad."

Groucho Marx

Let the Games Begin

"This is it" If you are new to the further-up-the-ladder side of life gang, at the peak of experience, anxious and antsy to begin retirement, welcome. These are the first weeks of a new venture into all those promises of free time, FREE TIME, and all the guarantees of bliss and tranquility. Life will be good. Life will be fun. Life will be all fun and games from here on out: Nothing but entertaining activities and that Clown smile will break out on your face from now on.

That's how it begins.

Soon, though, unfortunately, though, reality will hit you in the face like a whip-cream and Kiwi pie. Now what?

Below are some woeful hints that will elbow into your life and enlighten you with the reality that it's *Time for You to Have More Fun.* If any of the following listed habits or events creep into your lifestyle, it's a warning to hit the *Fun Button* ...

... in your brain and ride in front the engine of your life instead of the caboose watching the past go by.

Hints you need more Fun in your life?

- **?** If you have memorized the Prime Time TV timetable for the first seven days of the week.
- **?** If you dressed in your slippers and sweat suit when you rose in morning, and took them off at bedtime.
- **?** If you are aware of the refrigerator motor going on and off and begin to time it.
- **?** If you lose track for another time while counting the ceiling tiles.

- **?** If you measured your feet every day last week to see if they really are growing.
- **?** If a trip to the kitchen is your vacation and you take photos along the way.
- **?** If you steam your green peas one at a time.
- **?** If you forget what *it* is, and how to spell *s_x*.
- **?** If you have an on-going, intelligent conversation with your cat or goldfish and they answer back.
- **?** If you find yourself sitting on the bathroom stool and wonder why you are there.
- **?** Or if you venture into the garage and stand at the door, and can't quite remember whether you went in there for a tool or a drive to the mailbox.
- **?** If, after you have memorized the morning newspaper, you begin again taking on the task of counting your sox.
- **?** If today is yesterday all over again, and tomorrow you have the same things planned.
- **?** If you put new batteries in your TV remote so you can switch the channels faster.
- **?** If you ring your doorbell to find out if you are home ...
- **?** If you are talking to yourself and carrying on a two-part conversation.
- **?** If you think this two-part conversation is a social life.

If any of the above describes you, it is time to check the options on your fun list. It may come as a surprise how much is outside the front door beyond that doorbell.

Maybe filling out the '*Test for Fun' Questionnaire* at the end of the book on can help you spur up the juices and set the mood for the future based on the past.

? Who Shot JR?

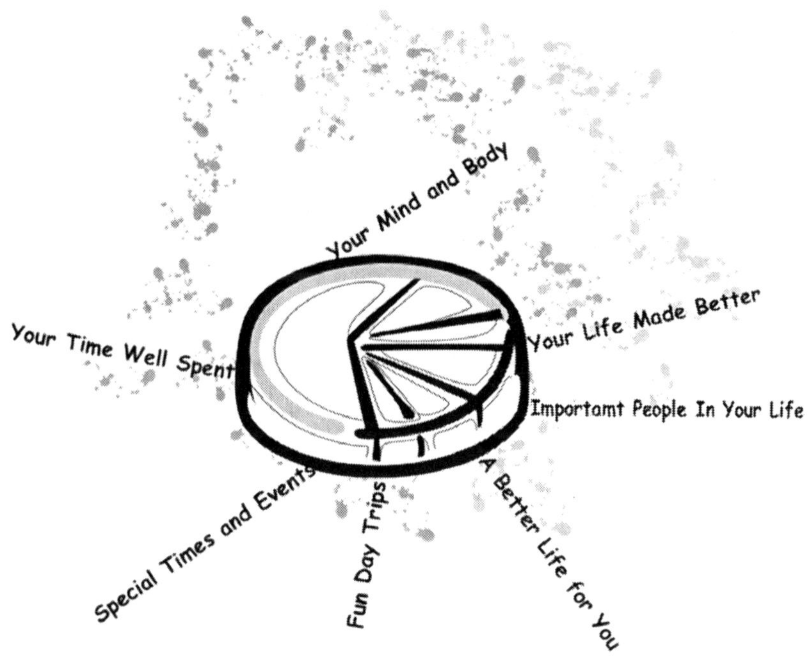

Slices of Life

(You must read these and sorta copy those seniors who have got there ahead of you).

The first thing you do is to examine and learn from the history and knowledge of others who have stumbled into retirement before you and have experienced the conversion bungles from work to fun. The following episodes and stories are divided into six sections that reveal actual and imaginary slice-of-life experiences that can complicate the everyday functions, trials and nuisances in retirement.

These slices of life are divided into the illogical sections: *Your Mind and Body; Your Life Made Better; Your Time Well Spent; Special Times; A Better Life for You;* and *Fun Day Trips*. These slices of Life are followed by relevant information and little known facts: *Important People; Traveling Seniors, and Dreams, Fantasies, Facts, Jokes, and Elucidations*. These events, circumstances and bits of trivial advice have already been tried-and-true ingredients of senior life somewhere, and can happen to any senior citizen anywhere who attempts to replace chaos, in a world of chaos, with the peace and serenity of a retired and well-deserved fun-filled life.

These events are sometimes greatly exaggerated and dramatized facts of retired life, but hidden between the lines are bona fide truths. The simplest things in life will become a matrix of unanswered questions if not approached as if you are gingerly walking across quicksand. One false step can suck you and today's retirement fun into yesterday's workday toil and trouble. You don't want that.

The things described here can happen ... and maybe they already have. Questions must be answered. Who are you? Where are you and if you move, how do you get there? And what do you do when you arrive? Is it safe to eat? Is it safe to drive? What do you want to be and with whom? Reading these stories and essays may ease some of the transitional bumps that appear to rock your winding road leading to leisure and fun.

? "You are about to enter another dimension, a dimension not only of sight and sound but of mind ... a journey into a wondrous land of imagination. Next stop______" – WHERE?

First: Your Mind and Body

Your *Mind and Body* are the first things you must take care of and put in order for that road down 'Fun with Retirement'. First, you must determine and qualify that you are *'All Grown Up Now'* and in fact ready and adult enough to qualify for retirement. Then you should leave the largest part of your past in that creased and crinkled photo album along with the *Would, Coulda, Shoulda* attitude and remember, memory lane is now a freeway into the future.

The Body must be able to take the pressure of wide grins and belly laughing as you spin through the retirement years. There are many things to consider: *The Body's Worth*; *The Aging Battle*; and *Being Silly is OK, too:* whether to transcend your mind and body through *Zen vs. Nap*; *Your Gastronomic Chemistry Set* will help analysis and forecast what you are dumping into your body through its mouth portal; *What is Eating Smart* and is it smart food; and remembering this retirement thing is *Not for Sissies.*

All Grown up Now?

Who are you? We know the definition of a teenager: that is, we human creatures who put up with all the trials and tribulations, the invasion of an acne army and moaning growing pains, between the ages of 13 to 19. We know a baby is a small human in diapers with an insatiable appetite, and a tweener is somebody between a baby and a teenager; 'too young for this' and 'too old for that'.

And it is assumed an adult is anyone with enough cumulative heartbeats to legally purchase and drink liquor, smoke cigarettes and gamble, be qualified to vote (if they want to), sign a contract, and do generally anything to enhance or defame the human image.

However, when are we officially considered a grown-up? That is the first question that must be acceptably answered in order to qualify for the rigors of passing into the retirement kingdom. You know; you must be someone who is full-sized, full-fledged, fully developed, both mentally and physically, and qualified for an enhanced lifestyle. Is that the qualification for retirement?

Moreover, is retirement the natural passage between adulthood and grownup hood? Is there another choice? There are so many things they didn't tell us when we were handed a birth certificate and declared to be a human, and this is one of those transparent smudges in life we cross with no instructions, or even a amusement-park-type map for directions.

Maybe people must qualify to be a grown-up: A test should be administered and passed before anyone can claim this status of nobility. To be really qualified I bet there are questions like: Do you know who *Rosie the Riveter* is and the *Yankee Clipper*? Do *Pearl Harbor* and *Air Raid Sirens* shatter your memories?

And to be a little less qualified I bet there are questions like: Can you define *'I like Ike', Rock Around the Clock*, *Ozzie and Harriet*, and the *Brooklyn Dodgers*? Do you remember dancing the *Twist* or the *Bunny Hop* in *Pegger pants*, or *pedal pushers*, and a turned up collar, and for some of us, with our greasy hair shining under the revolving mirrored globe hanging from the gymnasium ceiling, while listening to music on the Hi-Fi?

The physical qualifications are easier to ascertain. If your well-weathered face doesn't qualify for the cover of Elle or GQ magazine, you're in. Now you might be able to run a marathon race, but more than likely if your bones ache going from the front door to the car, you're in. If you believe gravity is the worst element in all of nature's wonders, and the southern environment sunshine is the best, you're in. If you purchase canned food and you quit purchasing food in jars because you can no longer open the lids with your hands, you're in.

Social qualifications take on the traits of a new Law hop scotching through Congress. What being grown-up is to one person is different to the next. (You see, lobbyists have already taken a nibble out of the process.)

Responsibility seems to loom as a defining guideline for grown-ups: Learning to take responsibility and consequences for your actions. Learning to treat people as you would like to be treated yourself. When you realize the entire world does not revolve around you and that it will go on tomorrow, with or without you, you are now socially a grown-up.

Come On! Is this grownup hood or the Boy Scouts?

Then other critical questions arise: Is anyone ever completely grown-up? Does everyone really want to be a grown-up? Do you have to go through all this trouble? Can you be grown-up and still be an adult and have the energy and attitude of a teenager? Maybe just being a plain old adult is better.

If you finally admit to being a grown-up, then will somebody fix the bathroom mirror that makes you look like your grownup father?

Senior Quote:

"It is absolutely wonderful to be so free and to have so many interesting choices to make about how to spend this time of life." ...

Emily: Richmond, VA

Woulda, Coulda, Shoulda,

(Or: Memory Lane is NOW a Freeway)

You probably have taken an exciting jaunt, as most of us do at one time or another, to the old fun spots you haunted in youth. You drove past the café where you drank Cherry Cokes while in high school, past the drive-in movie where you first made out, and then looked for the seedy bar where you sneaked your first under-aged beer.

And Whoa! A futuristic surprise, you found they are now a Starbucks, Wal-Mart, and Hooters, or worse yet, a used car lot. These aren't bad places, just not the warm fuzzy experience you were expecting. Face it, your memory lane is now a freeway.

30 or 40 years ago the world was a less complex place, easy going, or *cool*, whatever. Old European philosophers, who profess to know everything, including the ruts in life's road, have said, "*People are too soon old and too late smart.*" You've heard it all before, "I shoulda listened when I had the chance!" "I woulda done it differently if I had known!" "I coulda been a contendah!" You've probably said it all at one time or another.

"Take my wife -- Please," is a well-known Henny Youngman joke. How many have thought that quietly inside? Moreover, of course, the same is the case in a gender role reversal. One could alter it to, 'take my life', 'take my house', 'take my relatives and my friends – pleeeese', or even more introspective, "*Take this job and shove it!*" as stated in the Honky Tonk song by *Johnny Paycheck*. If only you had the nerve... to ...

News Flash: You can't be somebody else no matter how hard you try.

Let's face it, things haven't changed that much, it's just that the alphabet has been shuffled around: You wanted long hair, now you are longing for hair; Rolling Stones and now it's Kidney Stones; Whatever, Depends; Disco then Costco; then a BMW, now a BM; a new Hip Joint, now a new hip joint; KEG now EKG; and the best of all, trying to look like Marlon Brando or Liz Taylor, and NOW, trying NOT to look like Marlon Brando or Liz Taylor.

It's sad but true the Barber Shop and the barber have become a Solon and stylist; The corner Candy Store with its glass cases cluttered with mouth-watering sweets has become a 7-11 with racks of paper packs of candy you can't see until you buy; and City Parks are now drive-thru peek-a-view glimpses of the water out there somewhere, like a secretive UFO – you know it's there because you are told it's so.

It's a given that you can't stop the progress of the eternal timeline, but do you have to rub out the past so thoroughly? It's as if all the nice things you did were penciled in and the eraser has been rubbed down to the lead nib to kill the memory. You know you can't bring it back. Sorta like bringing South Dakota home in a suitcase after a glorious vacation there. But, if you really do want déjà vu experiences, then go to an antique shop, a classic auto show, or watch reruns of B&W movies.

At some point in life, most people wish they had done something they had instead passed up. They wish they could change it. But that's that, and to carry that baggage is a waste of time and blunts the mystery of the future. Do you really want to live all over again the life of being a teen with acne and glowing zits and a tie-down tux, or corsage and gown worn for the prom; living the life of *Ozzie and Harriet*; seeing *Elvis* when he really was alive and thin; listening to *Bill Haley* and *Rock Around the Clock*; and taking pictures with a *Baby Brownie Kodak*?

Well, maybe...

You woulda changed your life if you coulda known what shoulda been done different. You won't know now anyhow. So you might as well move on, enjoy the future, and try not getting stuck on the freeway.

? Who are Fibber McGee and Molly?

The Body's Worth

(Asset or Liability)

When you dripped out of the shower this morning and looked into that steamy full-length mirror, were you looking at an asset, or a liability? A while back an industrious senior friend and I were leaving the city dump and he asked the attendant at the scale, "What is the fee for dumping." She answered, "$20.55 per ton including tax."

That meant, my friend quickly figured, it would only cost a little over $2.00 to leave your body here at the city dump instead of disturbing the soil someplace. That led to a conversation and exploration into the value of a human body, that is, the entire material or physical structure of the organism humans carry around every day.

We found too many statistics and studies conducted to determine the chemical value of the human body. They range from the $.89 value we were taught in school, excluding of course the cost of extracting the elements, inflation and the fluctuating stock market for the price of chemicals, to a $4.50 value including the skin.

Apparently a Japanese team meticulously measured the square area of the skin on a human body and determined it was between 14 and 18 square feet; depending upon the body size. They also determined using the approximate price of quality cowhide, about $.25 per square foot, the skin of the human body averaged out to be worth about $3.50. Now that means the other day when I was participating in one of my asset building activities, softball, and I scrapped my rear sliding into second, it cost me a several pennies off my asset. The question is ... *'did that negate the afternoon of asset building.'*

This is a mere pittance of the real value. New studies have found a person can feel like 45 million bucks, instead of a million, on a good day. Replacement body parts are only a fraction of the value. A lung, heart or a kidney is worth only between $50 and $100 grand. The brain has no value, sometimes even an active one.

But throwing in the DNA, antibodies, male sperm, female eggs (here again women are worth more than men), and especially the bone marrow, these elevate the value up into the comfort zone, that is if you believe insurance companies and hospitals.

Put the items on E-bay and you will probably watch the value climb from the comfort zone to the stratosphere.

There is only one drawback to the economic process of this evaluation: All prices are based on living tissue and I do not know how long I could sit still for having the DNA, or other valuable cash producing things, extracted from my body, in-by-inch and molecule-by-molecule.

But getting back to earth, we had to determine whether the human body was worth more than a plug nickel other than to a chemist or surgeon. There are value scales other than the scientific. To fly your body from New York, NY to Melbourne, Australia and back, first class, makes your live body worth $16,906 to the airlines for taking up one seat on a 747. If you feel you have an economy type body, it's only worth $3,197 for a less comfortable seat. Being too close to the subject, we didn't venture to ask the cost of a departed body on the same trip.

To ride a bus it's only worth about a buck or so. To sit that same body in a VIP seat at the Broadway show, The Producers, for 2 hours and 40 minutes it will cost you $200 plus $40 service charge, whatever that is.

Looking at all the figures, it's determined that our body-asset is like a small business. Any balance sheet, even for our body-asset, has expenses subtracted from the actual value. We figured haircuts, perms, manicures, body waxing, cosmetics, shaving, some visits to the dentist, and the like, were minor maintenance expenses that improve the package, but not the product. Plastic surgery, we figured, was in a neutral zone between body maintenance and mental maintenance. Doctor appointments and operations were major and necessary maintenance expenses to keep our asset an asset and not a total liability.

Physically working out the body, in one form of exercise or another, was positively split between minor and major expenses; looking good on the outside, and feeling good on the inside ... with a dash of mental maintenance thrown in.

What to eat? What to eat? This is a totally different subject and deserving of a full examination. Nevertheless, in a nutshell, and by the way nuts are good for you and your cholesterol level, if you follow every recommended diet and believe every scientific study, you will wither your asset away from the confusion. How to exercise? That is another profit making decision to be studied in your spare time, and a personal preference.

The bottom line comes down to the fact that the body reflected in the steamy mirror is your primary asset and it must be taken care of while you haul it around. Eat correctly and exercise smartly and you have a long-term asset; do not and you have a short-term liability. Eventually, you know, you may be asked quit carrying it around and exchange it for a no-maintenance Casper-the-Friendly-Ghost type body that will not be reflected in the mirror. In the meantime, watch your asset.

? Who was Alben Barkley?

Quote:

I can't understand why I flunked American history. When I was a kid there was so little of it.

George Burns

The Aging Battle

(The immortality dream)

The anti-aging, age-defying, longevity, staying young, never aging, and the most extreme, the never-ever dying goals in life, have spawned industries that create solutions and concoctions that materialize in the form of lotions, oils, skin creams, growth hormones, mud baths, secret herbs, nutritional supplements, and laser beams, etc. They are short-term answers to the age-old problem of a longer life.

A little while back, another thorough and surely a painstaking study revealed that Americans spent $20 billion on various anti-aging products. To this date, there is absolutely no scientific proof that any commercially available product will stop time or reverse aging, no matter how many lobbyists the pharmaceutical companies put in Washington; of course, optimistically, anything can still happen in this scientific age, especially of the proper palms are greased.

Let us examine the core of the aging problem. There is only one legitimate, workable counter-attack in the battle against this process: Stop all the intimidating sweeping hands on clocks, especially the alarm type, and rip the calendar numbers off the walls. Ignore everything and anything that announces the date or time such as newspapers, TV and the Town Crier. Mainly, don't celebrate birthdays.

Age is the duration of time one has existed. After all, aging is in actuality the passing of time, is it not? That steady arrow that silently moves in an undisturbed motion invisibly passing in front of your eyes through life on ball-bearing castors. It's the movement of the planets and tides, hopeful buds popping from the earth in the spring and tree leaves drying in the autumn like weathered skin. It is the organic process of growing older and showing effects of increasing age. 'No time, no aging,' it's as easy as that. Unless science can stop time, you have a problem.

If Juan Ponce de León had in fact discovered the Fountain of Youth in Florida in about 1513, you wouldn't have to worry. If you had a portrait similar to the Dorian Gray picture that cracked, wrinkled and aged for you, you wouldn't have to worry. A sip of the elixir of life potion and the resulting immortality would be fun. But, NOT!

It is a fact and historical consensus proves it: Without a doubt, 9999 out of every 10,000 humans unsuccessfully inhibit the aging process. Moreover, that lonely one in 10,000, rumor has it, manages to beat the process and shows up as a same-old rehashed politician. The odds are against all of us: We either pass to the other side or become a politician.

As has been acknowledged, after all, aging is the organic process of growing older and showing the effects of increasing age; graying, wrinkling, sagging, and shrinking. However, there are some positive qualities to aging, like acquiring desirable qualities by existing left undisturbed for some time, you know, like good bourbon or tasty cheese, or becoming a ripe banana or pomegranate.

Maturing, as some people look at it, is the process of developing an entity until it reaches perfection. Somebody forgot to define perfection in the eternal human-life process. It can be anything in the eyes of the beholder in this twilight zone between being and not being.

The immortality dream can take on many concepts when mixed with personal and debatable reality. *"Do not go gentle into that good night. Rage, rage against the dying of the light,"* said Dylan Thomas. *"Time to turn back and descend the stair, with a bald spot in the middle of my hair--,"* said T. S. Eliot. These are observations on facing the phenomena of life and aging.

"Look younger," says every beauty magazine on the drugstore rack: This is nothing but sales gibberish. Unfortunately, eternal youth found in a bottle or a jar, or even in a poem, is but a myth perpetuated by the anti-aging agents of profit. But, anything can happen.

Becoming a robot is one way to attain perfection and beat aging, but how can someone walk in high heels or sneakers with those clubfeet. The touchy-feely part of life is discombobulated.

Wigs, weaves, plugs, dyes, skin grafts, wrinkle removers and plastic surgery do not make someone younger, but can make anyone feel younger. They come close to the ultimate answer: robotic renovation – that is, becoming a mechanical device that sometimes resembles a human and is capable of performing a variety of often-complex human tasks on command or by advance programming and manipulation.

You may have seen some individuals who feel plastics are fantastic and believe they will never die because they can never decompose. However, being a robot, or wanna-be robot, leaves out the option of tasting that fine bourbon and cheese, or eating a banana.

But again, something may eventually happen because you believe time is eternal, hope is not lost; maybe the scientific community of anti-aging gurus can clone time's eternal properties into the human DNA.

Who nose?

? Who is Pvt. Gomer Pyle?

Being Silly is OK, too

(Or: Laugh yourself to Health)

As we elbow our way toward a life based around easy-going and long-lasting coffee breaks, being silly is OK; after all, grandma often told us that laughter is good medicine and it keeps us healthy physically, mentally and socially; at least she should have. But it's not an easy task; being a clown or a card is hard work. It must be practiced every day ... and maybe every moment ... to keep a sharp edge.

And why is this important? Does it have benefits? Did you ever notice how the longevity of Hollywood seems to be a custom and maybe mandatory qualification in the world of comedians? Bob Hope and George Burns joked around for a 100 years, Milton Berle for 93, and Jack Benny at 80 and Red Buttons at 87 left laughing a little earlier, but beat the odds. They probably laughed themselves to health. *"Life is far too important to be taken seriously,"* said Oscar Wilde.

And don't let it trouble you if some question your new outward comic approach to life, simply beam a Mona Lisa grin and give them an Eddie Cantor eye roll. Learning to adopt a lighter outlook and seeing the funny side of everyday situations will give you the resilience you need to cope with those tough situations. 'I've seen it all,' you may respond, just don't let on that you can't remember it all.

You don't have to pedal your bike around town with a balloon attached to your bonnet as was recently reported. That was a little over the top ... so to speak. There must be a thin line between being silly, and being foolish. Being silly probably causes laughter, while being foolish may cause embarrassment or harm. Breaking out that toothy smile and a pleasant anecdote more often is a better option than planting banana peels along the sidewalk, or tossing water balloons from the window. That's kid's stuff ... but then again ...

But on a more serious note about being silly: less stress, more optimism; less anger, more joy; less anxiety and better health all around. Being a Cranky or Crabby person is like being the square peg at a round-hole party, you won't fit in at many places. The opposite of being silly is being logical, rational, reasonable, serious, sound, and weighty. The only things left out of this list are very starched collars and black garments. Cool, crazy, daffy, dippy, dizzy, wacky and colorful garments are more what you are looking for.

Mel Brooks, comedian, actor, and producer well into his 80s, believes that *"Humor is just another defense against the universe."* At every poll taken of residents at every Memorial park, everyone who responded agreed that humor probably would have given them a few more days. And they also suggested that you be nice to the people around you, they may be the ones who choose your eternal home.

The goal of having a sense of humor is happiness ... in and around us. It's not a new thing; Aristotle said back in about the 350BC days, *"Happiness depends upon ourselves."* We have to do it and make the effort.

Practicing a toothy grin in front of a mirror may work. After all, many TV news anchor people must do it daily: Keeping sharp by reading joke books and online gag sites must help. Exchanging jokes with friends by e-mail is a current activity done by many. Humor is everywhere and in everything and is an art that requires continuous tweaking and a love for people; and is not for those with over-sized egos.

Lots of times the result of your attempt at humor, the laughter you expected, may be replaced by a loud and collective groan. If there are no risks and chances taken, there are no rewards.

Silliness sometimes is its own reward, even when you are the only one laughing.

? What is Highway Patrol, who starred in it, and in what years?

Zen vs. Nap

A glazed donut smothered with dark chocolate and garnished with a rainbow of sprinkles vs. a sugarless/non-raisin bran muffin: Like asking yourself to choose between riding on a trike with a square front tire or in a stretch Limo with a complimentary bar.

Since exchanging your occupation-machine routine for a serene state of eternal retreat, you've had to make so many new choices between happiness and health ... 'one leads to the other', so you've been told ... but to you they're like animate forks in the road through life that interweave around each other. One leads to the other and they mirror each other just like a couple married for countless years.

How do you best really treat your body and mind to become a healthier and yet happier person? You go to the source, and politely ask your inner self ... who, unfortunately, at the time, is busy reading the TV schedule.

Meditation, of course, or Zen as some people call it, is a subject often linked to the state of true happiness (suggesting it is opposed to ordinary happiness being a small fib). Zen meditation refers to a condition in which the body is consciously relaxed and the mind becomes calm and focused: meaning, '*Continuous and profound contemplation or musing on a subject or series of subjects of a deep or abstruse nature*'.

This could easily describe your state just before you take an afternoon Nap on the couch. Do toes count as subjects of abstruse nature? A Nap, as you are aware, is *'a sleep for a brief period, often during the day ... to doze'*: and it has another meaning; *'to pour or put a sauce or gravy over a cooked dish'*. You could easily be a cooked dish when you vegetate on the couch during an afternoon siesta, but not for this purpose of pursuing happiness in the psychic sense.

After thorough research, you may come to believe the Nap option is closer to the phenomenon of meditation than most people believe. Both are approaches to true happiness, Zen and Nap; position the mind (and body) in a relaxed state in order to become calm and focused.

If you tell your friends you take a short Zen period every afternoon, then would that be far from the truth? In addition, you would appear to be a deep person since you are seeking happiness using a universal, trendy, contemplative method. Besides, Naps are not that far from true happiness. You do have free-flowing happy dreams in old style Technicolor while flattened on your back on the couch; although mostly in slow motion and vivid flashbacks, but unfortunately, you are obligated to sit in the senior discount seats.

Breakfast is another and the first genuine challenge in the choices between happiness and health during the day (besides pushing or not pushing the snooze button on the alarm). There is that bran muffin again. Add a bowl of oatmeal and black coffee and you have a breakfast as exciting as a one-horse race: How about ham or sausage or bacon, eggs, hash browns and toast. You can hover over this platter of happiness at least once a week at Ma's Café on the corner of cholesterol and glucose. You must admit, though, this weekly weakness trashes the health aspects of happiness, but nonetheless raises the joy-of-life happiness to a temporary level of ecstasy ... and nutritional nirvana.

You may have found, since allowed to make your own decisions and not wedged into a rut, seemingly commonplace everyday choices can be earthshakingly important options in the quest for a healthy and fun-filled happy life. (WOW! is that a mouthful of gingersnap words), such as 'to walk' or 'to drive' (depends on the weather); 'cola' or 'diet' soda; (with or without spirits); 'regular' or 'decaf'; or a few laps on the treadmill then a session of Tai Chi.

Now Tai Chi may be the ideal game and at your perfect speed ... slow, fluid and gentle, and practiced outdoors, that is, if you don't mind appearing like a fool. It's a physical meditation we're told. You've more than likely seen some of your neighbors practice it down the street in the park (it must be practice because it never looks completely refined). They say it can help with everything from blood pressure to increased bone density to lowering stress.

That is a lot to expect from an exercise imitating a stork stuck in the mud. They claim it gives them a better perspective of their life challenges and problems; and you can say that would be an indisputable fact each time they lose their balance and fall to the ground flat on their back. Everything looks up from down there.

However, you must return to the original question: How do you best treat your body so you become a healthier and yet happier person? In addition, your fence-walking answer is simple ... chocolate flavored bran donuts with raisins and sugarless sprinkles, followed by a dozing episode of Zen.

***Senior Quote**:*

The most fun thing I have done since my retirement? SEX ... The most surprisingly fun thing I have found out about retirement ... SEX ...new hobbies or activities after retirement, SEX ...

John: Vancouver, Canada

Your Gastronomic Chemistry Set

(The battle for the body)

Analyzing the components of what to eat using your gastronomic chemistry set is essential for concocting a wall of defense against the assault on your health or a longer lifespan. Being a senior citizen and wanting to graduate to being a wise old person is a constant challenge that makes it is necessary to carefully pick and choose your poisons.

It is full-time battle against all odds and involves not only the woeful time spent at the table, but also the pre-research and calculation processes you must perform to decide what and when to eat. If 5 good or bad for you, what it will cure, what it will prevent, and what body part will fall off or what will be added by its consumption.

You can prepare oatmeal for breakfast. It is a heart-healthy fiber that supports your body's fight against BAD cholesterol, and not because the glob in the bowl is a mouth-watering delicacy. You use non-fat milk because it is what it says it is, and instead of sugar, use just a *taste of honey*, since it is rich in antioxidants that prevent cancer and adds a golden color to the glob.

You probably remember when you ate honey just because it tasted good. You can add a few blueberries or raisins to the glob, if you have any; they also help fight the BAD cholesterol. "I know, I know" you may say, "but some of the affluent boomers can eat hand rolled Cheerios and freshly squeezed banana juice, but this glob is what I am stuck with."

Salmon also helps the heart, but you certainly don't picture yourself spreading it on top of oatmeal early in the day unless you include a squeeze of lemon. You can sprinkle a quarter teaspoon of cinnamon on the glob, which adds extra decorative color and improves the glucose metabolism, and prevents your body being taken prisoner by diabetes 2. You do all these things because you were told to do so by your supporting army of published nutritionists, and you add a glass of orange juice since it contains everything good, including the sun, as does any fresh fruit. It also lowers blood pressure.

You eat all your breakfast and feel invincible.

After the morning ritual of preparing breakfast, you realize the real-life normal function of food consumption has become a fundamental part of the entire day. Not surprising, since it happens at least 3 times, and takes up so much of your time and cash; eating has become a full-time struggle to protect the body against the invasion of bad things. Now none of us is an expert on nutrition (as opposed to well-practiced eaters), and certainly not a member of the accumulation of experienced researchers and nutritionists who rally around to protect the body, if you were you'd have to write a book to qualify, but you do bring that lifetime of eating experience to the table.

After oozing down your breakfast, you feel like a satisfied kid. You feel like a successful chemist. You also feel confused because lunch is just a few hours away. Lately the paranoid feeling that everything you consume is a life-threatening plot against your longevity. But, and you believe it as fact, this is not half as much fun as flirting with the server while downing hash browns, ham or bacon or sausage, and eggs and buttered toast. Many days you are tempted to sacrifice a few hours of the unknown future for a single meal of joy; and some days the temptation wins. However, do not tell anyone in your army who are battling the health baddies.

There are so many convoluting, contradicting, and proven studies and marketing statements that it's hard to boil them down to fit into an ideal, yet non-intrusive, nutritional lifestyle.

Let's take one good example, 'Cool ... Clear ... Water'. You have always been told to drink eight 8-ounce glasses (64 ounces) of water per day. Recently that has been revealed as a myth (probably started by well diggers), because you only lose about 1 liter (33.8 ounces) of water a day through sweat and bodily processes; about four glasses. What is the world coming to? If nutrition experts cannot figure out water, how can you believe them about steak? Then the questions arise, how much to drink, when, and what? When the time comes and you feel thirsty as a prospector in the Mojave Desert, they say you are already dehydrated.

In addition, they say, bottled water does not contain enough fluoride to prevent cavities in children (not your problem anymore), and some tap water contains health-harming bacteria or parasites. What a dilemma, bottle or tap? Bottle or Tap? A filtration system under the kitchen sink that performs reverse osmosis (RO) is a great answer while at home, but a better answer would be a RO built into your body so you can drink from a public fountain or out of the river. There is a $1,000,000 idea for some genius human-body technician.

The scariest part of the day: *What's for lunch?* Here your gastronomic chemistry set is used to analyze the rations you are about to eat, and choose what you will not eat. Hot dogs and the usual processed meats you consume between bread on sandwiches, besides being fattening, contain preservatives, additives, and other chemicals used for processing. They include toxic nitrates and nitrites, or chemicals formed during processing, and can pull the trigger of the gun aimed at your nervous system. They are also snipers in the body knocking off elements sensitive to insulin, and thus provide another chance of you being taken prisoner by Diabetes 2.

Soup is good, home cooked is better, and some in cans are OK, but there are so many flavors and recipes that thorough research is involved to avoid fats and retain nutrients. Eating fast food is a notoriously and highly publicized bad-bad no-no exposed for a multitude of chemical desperados. A salad bar never fails the fast food test unless it is loaded with pepperoni and sausage from the pizza bar, or covered with chocolate syrup from the desert bar.

Dinner can offer one gleaming hope in this siege against your body surrounded by an army of destructive elements. That is, if you avoid red meat and pork, which poke red flags along the colon; pizza, which has more artery hardening fat than a cheeseburger; and potatoes, which are good, but with butter or gravy are fattening. Pasta carries a guarantee to make love-handle bulges on your sides.

Chicken and turkey sans fatty skin (and not on pizza) are OK if not deep-fried in bad oil or smothered in a fattening cream sauce. Fresh vegetables steamed or slightly boiled are good chemicals but taste like vegetables that are steamed or boiled, again, no butter. Fresh vegetable salads are the best if tainted with vinegar and olive oil.

Dessert is just fine as long as it is non-fat, non-sugar, non-white flour, and served with the perfect taste and texture of cardboard or Plaster of Paris. Dark chocolate contains those helpful antioxidants. What can be said about Jell-O?

Your gastronomic chemistry set, as you see, is merely a lifetime of knowledge collected over the years in your fight for life. After a while, it becomes a habit, and it should be, sort of like breathing ... and that is not a bad idea either.

? What did Ray Kroc launch in 1955?

The Miracle Cure-All

(Or: step-by-step to health)

You know all there is to know already. You discovered how to achieve it as a toddler, after trial and error, and for most of us, it has stuck in our memory and muscles. It's as easy as 1-2-1-2, except of course, when you must work around little aches and pains, maybe a bad knee or hip, or worse, one leg that has a mind of its own. Why, you remember don't you, years ago, it made man the superior and the more advanced of all animals.

What's the big deal about it? What's hard – put one foot in front of the other. That's not really a miracle of divine proportions. It's really a down-to-earth activity that even you can do ... and should do more of.

There are a variety of styles of this cure-all: ambling, strolling, strutting, shuffling, swaggering, skipping, speeding, pacing, marching, hiking, and more. Yes, you guessed it. So put on a pair of old shoes, hang the car keys in the closet next to your snack pack pudding, and start ... walking ... step-by-step to health.

You don't have to be one of those suckers (that is, other people, certainly not you) who spend $4.9 billion on exercise equipment. Be one of those 17% who are actually exercising today. You can go as far and as fast as you want ... around the block once or twice, around the neighbor hood, down one of the gazillion walking trails people plow through cities, or go downtown and do some speed-walk window shopping. You know what? Some people, on rainy days, speed walk around the mall before the glittering goods galleries open. Check it out.

So what does this cure-all cure or how does it help us? Read any magazine in the doctor's office as you wait to have your weight checked. There are tons of inks spread across Paul Bunyan's paper products describing and analyzing its benefits. It controls: that weight; blood pressure; heart problems; muscle tone; diabetes; lung capacity; metabolism; breast cancer; colon cancer; and even pot-belly-obia and fat-hips-itus.

So, how to start? Well, the most obvious and deeply profound answer is, "A journey of a thousand miles begins with a single step," said Confucius. That's a bit too far for your first stab at it. But a shallower answer is to find a reason, a goal, a justification, a driving inner force (such as a walk to the nearest Espresso Shop for a caffeine boost), or a walking partner ... even your dog will do, but not the cat because soon walking will become chasing.

Pretend you're going to the nearest fast-food-factory, but you're not going in ... and don't. Head for the strip-mall drugstore to get those aspirins you're going to need at the end of the journey. There are a million reasons to walk and only a couple not to: laziness and procrastination.

And the easy part, you can do it at your convenience: Instead of lunch, before breakfast, after dinner, during Oprah if you don't like the guest, or just after an argument for therapy as well as exercise. Did you know walking at a moderate pace for 30-60 minutes burns stored fat and can build muscle to speed up your metabolism. Walking an hour a day is also associated with cutting your risk of the multitude of health-threatening conditions listed above. Isn't it time to work 1-hour walks into your busy lifestyle?

There are a few little things that can be considered to augment the benefits and make the walk easier. Walk with weights (even two cans of soup will do) in your hands or on the ankles (not the soup).

Get a pedometer. It senses your body motion and counts your footsteps. This count is converted into distance by knowing the length of your usual stride. Wearing a pedometer and recording your daily steps and distance is a great motivating tool. Keeping a daily step-count log may sound stupid, but it provides you with a visual target and bragging-right proof that you are doing what you say.

Did you ever think about making those cell-phone calls to friends while you are walking, and not while driving? Think of the lives you'll save ... besides your own.

There you have it. The most advanced animal on the planet must go back thousands of years and restore the forgotten, but the easiest, cure-all miracle.

Not for Sissies

(Or: you don't have to think old.)

This aging thing is not for sissies. But, we do recognize that *we ol' folk* like to frequently talk about our health anyway. Only a few of the very barely healthy make it over the edge to a *C-note* in age, so any honest exchange of antidotes and anxieties with peers is a positive step toward that goal, as well as developing the art of not falling apart. Misery loves company, as well as an understanding ear.

After the regular annual checkup we all find everything is about the same, you know: cholesterol and blood pressure are still a little too close to the moon, blood sugar looks like a banana-split sundae; and the aches and pains of arthritis should be an acceptable punishment for all the good years, but aren't.

After they took your head out of your backend and reattached it to your neck, the doctor probably prescribed a reverse position so you can always see where you've been rather than where you're going ... something about the past being brighter and more upbeat than the future, or something like that, very encouraging words ... you probably vowed then and there to get this health thing under control.

Riiiggghhht!

At least we've got the past in our rear view mirror, where it belongs. The solution: It's said that keeping active like walking helps ... forward if possible ... and keeps those muscles and bones loose and lubricated, even though they hurt in strange and previously unknown places. Be sure to take the blood thinning and thickening pills the doctor gave you, those that battle the bad carbs, and especially those little devils that kill the pain. They all help us from becoming sobbing sissies about this aging thing.

We know, or we're told, life begins at 40, sometime in the distant past, but we also become aware that we're entering the 'initial' state of the golden years (SS, CD's, IRA's, AARP), but who said life was going to be uncomplicated and not scary? There are hurdles at every stage of life: Remember uncontrollable bowel movements as a baby; acne and raging hormones in the teens; misplaced *love* in the twenties and maybe the thirties; weight gain in the forties; and loss or graying of hair in the fifties ... just remember, a bald head is better than no head at all ... and then there's now.

Forget it and don't become overly concerned about body alterations and malfunctions, you know, like modified plumbing and body parts; fresh bone construction that will be an inconvenience; eyes that become windows to a fuzzy world; sounds disappearing behind a muffler; the constant reek of Vap-O-Rub and Absorbine Jr. following like a stalker; becoming wrinkled, saggy and lumpy, and that's just the left leg; and leaving your teeth in a glass and ears and eyes in a drawer when you go to bed. It's part of life.

It could be worse. We could go through those first 50 or 60 years all over again ... oh the pain of it ... the thought of it ... just makes us want to grin and bear these physical setbacks. As Golda Meir said, "Tough it out, what other choice do we have. Old age is like flying through a storm. Once you're aboard, there's nothing you can do." "But, must the storms erupt in my body," most may lament.

Get over it, millions if not gazillions of folks through the ages have passed through this storm and landed at the other end on both feet firmly planted, somewhere.

Bear in mind, you can't take it with you, but you can keep it as long as you can. And you just can't stop the aging process, but you don't have to think old. In order to change we must be sick and tired of being sick and tired.

Eating Smart

(Does that mean eating Smart Food?)

We know eating smart is the current health fad pounded from magazines, infomercials, PBS, and an occasional snake-oil salesperson who passes through town, gathers a crowd, charges a fee, spouts some gibberish, and tries to sell us a book or CD. Does that mean eating Smart Food?

What is Smart Food? Are we to eat Rhodes-Scholar rutabagas, or PhD peas, or morsels of IQ like iron or iodine spread over Quail or Quiche: So many decisions beyond that great bacon-burger with cheese served at the local drive-in?

On the more serious side, a colorful collection of graphs, charts and pyramids bloom and are printed in all the mags and rags on a regular basis that categorize and dramatize all the food qualities recognized by man. You should be familiar with these. It must be some kind of rule for prolonged existence. They have been cranked out by the government, as well as other health and profit minded parties, to educate us eaters on the benefits of eating correctly, thus living longer, slimmer, and more productive lives. (This is important to the government because it collects most of its taxes from living humans.)

Humans, and sometimes our pets, are the logical targets of this information bonanza because most of the other animal groups have their diet thoroughly and naturally figured out without this by-the-numbers education. They munch through it on a daily basis. Giraffes chomp on treetops and lions gobble up giraffe meat. Big fish eat little fish: It's a cliché as well as a fact.

The animal kingdom has a regular diet program called a *food chain* that has evolved and been tested through the ages; and it works. Most animals are still alive and eating, reproducing on a regular basis and looking darn healthy. And to be perfectly clear, in this definition Taco Tommy's just off the freeway is not considered a food chain.

Eat to live longer is the complete notion, but isn't that a given? If you stop eating, you die! Even a pretzel-poppin' nincompoop knows that! It is a simple nutritional reality known since the Garden of Eden. Why were the first people on earth placed in a garden of smart food (and not at a drive-in), and it was also occupied and shared by the original snake oil and apple salesman? It was a tempting taste of the future.

But let's get back to that bacon-burger with cheese and stack it up against the *Smart Food Guide Pyramid* pushed by the government and its allies. First, you start from the bottom, the bread layer: The burger has that, twice, two buns, another on the top. Bread is recommended by the perfect-food pyramid and is packed with complex carbohydrates and essential vitamins, though it calls for whole wheat instead of white bread in the pyramid; it is close but not with the full nutritionists blessing.

The next level up is the vegetable group. You can unquestionably confirm that the burger stacks up well against the pyramid in this layer: All those garden bits and pieces like onions, tomatoes, lettuce, pickles, ketchup, mustard, and maybe a gas-blasting jalapeno. What a potpourri of healthy stuff, i.e., smart food: A regular Garden of Eating.

Meat and cheese overwhelmingly satisfy the next level of the pyramid. A quarter pound, or more, of ground meat, and a serving (or two) of American cheese, provides a daily supply of all the carnivorous protein, vitamins and nutrients needed by man's body since menus were illustrated cave drawings of food on the run.

OK, now holding to the pyramid pattern, neatly placed at the top of the perfect-pyramid burger is a serving or two of bacon. It contains a little meat burnt to the proper charcoal level, and a little oil (grease) to assure things run smooth. Also lurking at the top of the pyramid are the sweets and spices, because you know that any reputable burger bar has mixed in a hefty helping of sugar and salt into that special sauce used for added flavor.

There it is. You can find smart food anywhere if you look hard enough with a vivid imagination. The conclusion you must come to is that a bacon-burger with cheese served through a window is in effect *smart food*, but the party pooper group of three-piece-suit nutritionists from the USDA recommend it as a dish only 2 or 3 times a month, not a day. Now that's dumb.

Who wants to endure a burger famine for 27 days a month just to stay healthy? Anything sounds better than Rhodes-Scholar rutabagas, which any breathing human animal would probably eat only 2 or 3 times a year, and try finding a drive-through supply of that stuff just down the street.

Smart Food is a smart idea for people who have the time to investigate it, cook it, eat at a kitchen table, and write a book or tape a video, but should only be a life-surviving hobby for those of you who want to live longer and healthier, in the animal kingdom group referred to as Homo sapiens.

Quote:

"As a child my family's menu consisted of two choices: ***take it*** *or* ***leave it****."*

Buddy Hackett

Second: Your Life Made Better

Location, Location, Relocation, to move or not to move, that is the question. Life should be more fun than living in neutral gear while sitting in your Ferrari. We are talking about the placing of that recliner chair near a golf course, a movie theater, and a shopping mall.

After having made the decision to move there is the problem of moving that hodgepodge of memories called your *Packrat Assets* and then dealing with the leftovers by creating a *Yard Sale for Fun and Profit*? When you've arrived at your location for the future fun, you will probably have left behind *Life' Life Savers'* type friends who you knew and depended on, and you may also have to find out *How to Live on $45 per Day* if you are on a limited income. And, after you finally plant your TV in the corner, you must determine whether it is really you who has arrived, because *Stolen Identity* can make you not you when you arrive. Your *Seventh Sense of Seniors* has been developed to keep you balanced and safe in all these comings and goings.

Location, Location, Re-location

(To move or not to move, that is the question)

Where are you going? Some people might think by location we are describing the permanent position of your cloud-like recliner, its proportionate alignment, and more importantly, its relationship and visual path to the never-never land behind the TV; as well as being geometrically positioned at the intersection of all noise being projected from the sound-system speakers. Kidding aside, this IS a significant lifestyle decision when considering where you want to be many years from now; but it is only part of the equation.

Life should also be more fun than living in neutral gear while sitting in your Ferrari.

Others may think this is a dialogue about the location of a white, dimpled, little hard ball after it has jumped off a pine tree into the rough and is laying on the ground, in the grass, perpendicular and closer to a little hole in the middle of a grass table, (some call it a 'lie', but we say 'location'). Then some in the entertainment industry are dreaming about movie sets when we mention 'location', and those in commerce who buy and sell bits and pieces of stuff may suppose we are considering a prospective sucker, excuse please, customer base.

Nope, none of the above: We are talking about the placing of that recliner near a golf course, a movie theater and a shopping mall. That is, the location of your soon-to-be domicile of leisure and relaxation from this day on. When we retire, we move, or most of us do. It seems to be a law of survival of some sort: like a moth being attracted to the heat of a light bulb, or as in some disastrous cases an active flame, we tend to follow the sun.

Change is not always bad; sometimes it is really only a horrifying process. But it is an essential decision that can influence your future wardrobe and the newspaper you read every day for the next 20 years or so.

The historical dream is rocking in a chair on a porch while soaking in the year-round sun, wading in the surf while inhaling ocean air, or reading a book, or playing checkers or golf with the neighbor; then you're hit it the face with a nine iron of reality.

You may actually find you are soaking in the smog-filtered sun and inhaling the cut-it-with-a-knife air of the industrial age; reading a book online; surfing the net and not the tides (it is a long walk through traffic from the deck to the ocean's surf). But the real, real nightmare, there are no more porches; they have followed the Edsel and TV's Highway Patrol into the sunset; only decks on the side of the building exist these days. Careful thought must be put into the type of air you breathe from now on, and where you will place that lawn chair, or rocker.

Moving to maybe-warmer weather and down sizing from a luxury level to a more comfortable level and leaving behind a lot of doodads is a hard decision. Or maybe like some citizens, just deciding not to move and staying in one of the snowbound areas of the world, which is just as appealing to only these few; especially those inclined to believe that snow and being ice-cold nine-months out of the year are invigorating (sort of like the occasional root canal). It is a difficult decision, almost as hard as *"Less filling? – More taste?"*

Really, though, it is an unproven fact that most people would rather be warm than cold, unless they want to carry a carton of ice cream or a TV dinner in their pocket or purse.

Then there are the fence walkers, or euphemistically called, snowbirds, who chose the best of both worlds; that is, eating tacos in the winter and fish and chips in the summer. This is the copout decision between change and continuity, choosing both. Or the genuine victims of wavering (and possibly the most adventurous of us) choose life on the road forever in an RV; wherever they park, that is where they are.

Seriously though, on the side of marginal common sense, some things should be considered before the Big Move; so many questions should be asked: What do you want to do when you grow up? Do want to call yourself Retired or Semi-Retired? Do you want to retire at all? Do you really want to be near your irritating family and friends, or only put up with them when you have to? Do you desire to live on Fantasy Island or Devil's Island? Can you solve crossword puzzles while wearing a parka and muffler? Do you want to appear tan and healthy, or white on white? How about swing dancing or a walk down the beach or up a hill?

Just make lists, and check them twice; it's easy. Make two columns: *Why You Want to Stay Here*, and *Why You Want to Go There*, and while making the list be as honest as your in-laws. And throughout this re-location process you can simply follow the advice of the philosopher/writer, Mark Twain, *"A man cannot be comfortable without his own approval."*

Packrat Assets

(Moving our hodgepodge of memories)

At some time most of us must make the decision. We consider moving shortly after we withdraw from our labor for subsistence. We have to make our change of days complete. It is the financially advantageous thing to do, we hope, and maybe a good thing, too, we justify. That is, the dreaded act of relocating from your Colonial full-family model 4-bedroom 1.5-bath middle-class home.

You have stuffed your home with a hodgepodge of memories stacked and stored in many closets, bedrooms, an attic, a basement, a garage, a yard, and a myriad of dusty nooks and crannies, all in a nice lawn-groomed neighborhood. Now you are considering a move to a downsized dwelling in another neighborhood with homes stacked one on top of the other with less space. It will make you happier; you fanaticize, and give you more time to do the things you want to do; you anticipate. You can finally de-clutter your life; you are sure.

It is an intimidating chore, this moving thing, you soon discover. Somehow, after all these years, your collection of memories has magically materialized into solid and heavy structures and shapes, and just possibly, there aren't enough boxes on earth to transport them, or a truck strong enough to drag away this bulk called your packrat assets. In addition, concurrently, putting toothpaste back into the tube comes to mind. Some memories will have to be forgotten, and some run through the trash compacter and shredder and others just abbreviated into smaller packages.

The unpacked boxes in the attic have gathered generations of dust, having been there since your previous move. You will strongly consider leaving them unopened and add them to the charity pile near the curb, or, unopened, dump them in the garbage. And then alas, what are you going to do with the semi-rusty garden tools and a gas-eating, smoke-spewing lawnmower, let alone the snaking never-could-coil-it-anyway rubber hose? You can't water and mow the carpet in your new and tinier abode.

You know why you kept the photos and artwork, but why the 1987 phone book, and TV Rabbit Ears? You must have considered at one time stuffing them and hanging them on the wall as a souvenir of the first boob tube in a long line of boob tubes that have possessed you in your lifespan.

More books than shelves. It is an accepted extraterrestrial law (which is more powerful than Murphy's Law) and known by cosmic travelers for eons, that whenever someone moves from one space to another space the books that fit in those shelves before, don't anymore. We should begin to tell small children to read a lot and read everything, but give away the books when you're done with them.

You must also determine if all the T- and Sweat-Shirts, baseball caps for the *Grateful Dead,* and *Give Peace a Chance,* and other advertising infinitum souvenirs, and so forth, are all worth moving again: Especially since they are quite a few sizes too small to ever wear again and are in the basic condition of cleaning rags. Moreover, as you look at your other rags (clothes) you decide you have stockpiled too many coats and sweaters for the warm weather environment, and are head-nodding affirmative in your belief that you purchased shoes by the pair and not by the dozen. Rabbit genes are involved here somehow, you are positive.

Additional cardboard moving boxes are always available at any of the local truck rental spots. They are sold in multiple sizes and shapes for encasing any conceivable item and cost from $1.10 to$7.25 each. The key here is to be certain that what you pack in a box is at least worth the price of the box or you are losing money.

In addition, this poses another hitch: Establishing the difference between assets and junk is like defining the difference between a rock and a boulder, and you have found, all possess the same properties of being equally dirty, ugly and heavy.

A yard or garage sale is out of the question. Many of these small items are only as valuable as the memories attached to them, and you must conclude that those are not saleable. You will find that your boxes and piles of donations to charity are slowly growing at the curb into an estate of its own, and that is a good and benevolent thing. You will see a bird picking pieces out of a wicker chair to build a nest, and are pleased that some part of it will be useful in a new home.

They say the earlier years of life lay the foundation for the later years and it is important to build on that foundation.

'They' who say that most likely have not moved their assets lately.

Quote:

Adversity makes men, and prosperity makes monsters.

Victor Hugo

Yard Sales for Fun and Profit

Finally, the apples of your eye have moved on to clutter up their own homes, and you are thinking about moving to smaller and cleaner abodes, or southern and warmer climates. It's the natural order of life. And this without a doubt may mean a yard or garage sale, to clear out your own clutter, and must be considered.

As enterprising citizens with the genes of a pack rat, you must scatter your treasures atop folding tables and across lawns to grudgingly part with precious icons from your materialistic histories. But first, you should examine this commercial experience so you can understand it, and possibly make it a constructive and profitable event. You need a plan that will be meticulously crafted and followed, and probably just as meticulously abandoned. There are several areas to be scrutinized before setting up this scavenger boutique, and a little hesitant advice may help.

Poster Fun: Hanging the letter-size posters on bulletin boards, utility poles and at bus stops is a ritual before any yard sale. But first, so many important decisions must be made before the hanging begins. What to call it?

Junk Sale sounds too trashy. *Closet Clutter Sale* sounds too desperate. *Good Stuff for Sale* sounds too iffy. *Pre-used Trash Sale* sounds too honest, and too negative, and definitely not very inviting. And *Pre-loved Trash Sale* sounds too cute.

Let's just call it a *Yard Sale* to keep it simple and within the easily recognizable universal language framework of all North American dwellers.

Directions, or a map, or an address are all options to be included on the poster if you want the drivers, or even the occasional walker, to arrive. Bright-red arrows painted on cardboard and hung on telephone poles on the nearest busy street are a big help. Make sure they are visible to the street, and the wind hasn't blown them upside down. An ordinary cardboard box with painted sides can work just as well if well placed on a center divide of a nearby road. Also, an A-frame sign on the curb in front of your house can stop any car. No need to put chains or a cable across the road.

Money: Pennies on the dollar is a fair swap for your time and material while planning for your less-than-cluttered future, and is a straightforward and obvious motivation for a Yard Sale. Money may be a crass commodity, but let's place it side-by-side for a fundamental value comparison with that collection of scratched-up tumblers, a gift from your great-grandma, with three missing. There is no material comparison. Money weighs less than old glasses, takes up less room, doesn't break, may be folded, and may again be swapped for replacement clutter. Great-grandma probably isn't with you anymore, so the glasses can go, for the right price, or any price, as far as that goes.

And what to charge for those items, you may ask? She probably paid thirteen bucks, you'll offer them for a buck, but take half-a-buck. It's a precise course of shrewd business planning called give-and-take. *You give me anything, and I'll take it.* Now, larger items are a little harder. A small sofa you purchased new for 600 bucks is really worth only about 150 bucks before the seller's markup, so the asking price is intuitively calculated to be 50 bucks if the buyer hauls it, but you will take 30 bucks just to get rid of it. It is all part of the *give-and-take* master business plan of all Yard Sales.

And how much change should you have on hand? How about accepting checks? Do you take them on trust, ask for ID, take fingerprints, ask for collateral, or not take checks at all? It's your money, so you decide. If you have any doubts, since it is all junk anyway, (unused items anyway) if the check doesn't clear you still have a positive transaction because the scavenger (customer) has carted away another unwanted, unused item that was taking up space in your garage.

Pre-Planning: If you've really thought ahead to the unmentionable, that is, the reality that some items might not be on the Yard Sale shoppers' list, then you have already called an organized charity to haul (pick up) the remaining items away. And then you find out, My God, even the most desperate charitable organizations will refuse to pick up some of your items! Un-usable! Un-sellable! This stuff really may be junk! And then you find out, of all things, that these organizations specialize, or have a list of items they *do* and *do not* take. One doesn't take TVs, another takes only clothes, another takes furniture but not lamps and kitchen items, and another specializes in broken items so they can teach trainee repair people. To do it right you would need a half dozen charities lining their trucks up in front of your house like a Mercy's Parade.

Physical Layout of the Sale: If it rains, what do you do? How do you post the prices? Big? Small? Or none at all? Everything listed as OBO (or best offer)? Or should you have a secret price list that only you know about and can reference? How many tables do you have? Need? Should you put mats down on your beautifully manicured lawn so it won't look like a cow pasture the next day? Should you open the garage door and put stuff in there? When should you open? Close? Should you serve snacks? What if no one shows up, what do you do?

All these are legitimate multiple-choice questions with so many answers they can't be listed here. The only answer is, *Figure it out!* That's the fun of holding a Yard Sale. (There it is again; that word 'fun'.)

Be careful of friends helping: A reminiscence here from an experienced yard sale authority, "I let a friend take over for me and when I came back from lunch, he proudly told me he had sold several of the old LPs, and the toolbox. I said *Great, How much did you get for the toolbox?* It was loaded with old tools I wouldn't be using anymore, probably a couple-hundred-bucks worth, and I had it marked for $100 OBO. He said, *five bucks*. I said *what? It was marked for $100 or best offer*. He said *5 bucks was his best offer*. And I fainted." Make sure the rules are clear, and one rule is clear; do not give things away ... unless they have a large truck with a detachable dumpster.

The Inventory: Rule One – Everything goes if you are moving out of town. Remember the old axiom, *'We always move more books than bookshelves.'* Well, it should be an old saying of some kind, some place.

Rule Two – Everything worthless goes if you are staying in town. *Use* and *Useful* and *Useless* are conditions that must to be defined by the seller, not the buyer.

Some have suggested that all your items should be cleaned and polished. That sounds like a lot of work, time, and more expense. Another option is to leave all that clean-up stuff to the buyer. That's part of their fun (there's that word again). Besides, whenever someone purchases an item from a Yard Sale, they always want to clean all your germs off and replace them with their own. It gives the item more of a personal touch.

The Customers: Some early arrivers are looking for that unnoticed antique article, or a piece of rare Renaissance artwork they can snap up for a few pennies and a belittling snicker. What can you do about it? Be shrewd and ask a little more for the item? Do nothing? Remember that a sale is a sale, and you never would have known anyhow that Aunt Minnie's needlepoint was really the hammock used by Lady Godiva after her infamous horse ride.

The bargain hunters, the wheeler-dealers, the price whittlers, the I-want-something-for-nothing shoppers will make your day. They bring the real spirit of a Greek Market with them. The best solution is to participate in the game with them and negotiate, and make the sale with a win-win result. It just feels good to bicker with a person one-on-one instead of handing a bar-coded plastic artifact to the clerk at the local discount store.

The real shoppers are the young mothers and fathers or living-together couples setting up a new household; also the teenagers who have finally been kicked out of their nests by their parents. These are bona fide customers. They have a limited vocabulary, though. *'How much is that?'* and *'Can I have it for a little less?'* And they have a limited bankroll, but they have an empty house or apartment to furnish and about half of everything you display is needed.

The Fun is Over: After the Yard Sale is over, there are going to be plenty of items (junk) left over that even the most addicted Yard Sale shopper couldn't purchase. Now the normal definition of a mystery is something not understood or beyond understanding. But we should all know there is no mystery here. It's a reality the dust gathering process will restart with a vigorous flamboyance enhanced by the parting potential customers spinning their tires in the dirt driveway. And a further reality will be revealed, as the sun sets, that all this time, unknown to you, all your precious icons of personal materialistic history are just dust magnets attracting all the particles from the cosmos. You probably will have to move them in a pack of trucks to the dust magnet headquarters, which is called the dump.

Ready! Set! Sell!

? What is the name of the princess on Howdy Doody Time?

Life's Life Savers

(Or: Don't forget those lesser best friends)

If you relocate, escape to the land of sun, fun, to enjoy the fruits of your life's labor, the move you've been planning for years, you'll be leaving a lot behind besides that brick Bar-B-Q in the back yard you can't stack in the truck. Your family, friends, maybe your doctor (who will probably be only a phone call away anyway) and your minister, rabbi or priest, who will always keep you in their prayers as they think of you, or maybe your wallet, at certain times of the years ... none these people will be lost forever.

But ... what about all those other very essential hometown people you've dealt with on a daily basis and who make life enjoyable, and even tolerable, and occasionally save your social life? Who's going to take their place? You know, such as the paper guy/gal who leaves the world within an arms reach at your front door every day. It's been an acceptable and no-brainer routine for years. And along the same train of thought, how about that faceless individual who magically makes envelopes and magazines materialize in your mailbox? Well, maybe you can do without the bills for a spell.

You'll have the new task to quickly replace these lesser best friends in your new pursuit of a comfortable life. Think about it.

Your barber or beautician

How long did it take you to hunt down and train that correct and talented hair artist who periodically makes you look and feel like a better human being, as well as being your confidant and confessor? How many bad-hair days did you endure until you successfully walked out their door with neat locks and tresses you could be proud of? This is an important part of your image, your hair, and what will be your look be after trying to train a new one for several weeks ... or months.

And that auto mechanic who knows your car(s) inside and out like a valued friend and can fix a clatter, squeak, or leak without breaking your bank. Do you remember how many hose jobs you got before you found this greasy knight who rescues your auto anxiety from the road of the unknown? And the first thing he said to you? "I tell my new customers, calm down, and don't break the fifth commandment, T*hou shalt not love thy cars more than thy wife and children*". He knew.

Then there's the barkeep you've trained to call you by your first name and plop your favorite drink, in front of you, before your backside finds comfort. He knows all your secrets, emotions, history, and more important, your tolerance level. He's probably the only person who's seen you cry. How can you replace this in just a few short days or nights? No way.

Next there's doctor's best friend and your personal handwriting decoder, your pharmacist, who actually knows what's going on inside you. He knows all the secrets, like, what to rub in your hair and not on your teeth, violet hair is not natural unless you used food dye instead of conditioner, and aspirin is the only bona fide miracle drug because it has cost about the same for years. How are you going to easily replace this knowledge bank?

How can you find a substitute for that syrupy smile that glows from the mouth of the corner-store clerk? She's been around for years and knows all the local gossip and isn't shy about revealing it all as you add a few more items to your shopping list. You go in to buy a few quick snacks for the big game, but also leave with snacks for the kids. She IS the big game, but it's worth it to find out who's married, and who's not.

There are so many of these essential modest life savers around that make living livable, they are hard to number, and difficult, and nearly impossible to replace in a strange land, a daunting thought. Think of your dentist, the gang at the coffee shop, and the lady at the dry cleaners who's been in your pants more than your mate. If you could just throw them in the truck with your memorabilia, you probably would, but no, unfortunately, you can't. Just don't forget them ... and good luck replacing them. But then again, maybe you should stay home ... or think of it as a new adventure in the sun.

Quote:

Friendship isn't a big thing - it's a million little things.

Author Unknown

? What came into existence between 1946 and 1964?

How to Live on $45 per Day

(And still have Fun)

Once upon a time there was a book called, *'Europe on $5 per day' by* Arthur Frommer. Those were the happy days. It's currently in the range of $70 per day. Taking that formula further into today's economy, living on $45 per day in retirement in the U.S. and having fun at the same time is a bona fide stretch, even by any miser's imagination. However, of course, we are considering one person. If there are two of you, you can probably skimp by on about $65. Half the world ... nearly three billion people ... lives on less than two dollars a day. That's not funny, and it's not a fair comparison because they don't have to pay $5 for a paper cup of coffee.

$45 was not a number picked out of the air. It is based on about the high payment made to a retiree from Social Security if it is taken at full retirement age.

How do you live on $45 per day?

Move if you are renting.

Doing some fingers-tapping research and based on 2006 prices, the average rent in Miami, Florida for a 2-bedroom apartment is about $1000 per month, in Las Vegas $830, Seattle $1025, Baltimore $995, and so on. That's not funny, either. Let's hope your house is paid for and the property taxes are low. That would be fun.

If you want to live economically in the Western U.S. the lower rents are: Tucson offers the least expensive apartments at an average of $616; Colorado Springs an average rent is $709; Boise, Idaho's average rent is $706; Salt Lake City is $680 and Albuquerque is $666.

It's a little tougher to live economically if you want to stay in, or move to, the Eastern U.S.: Indianapolis, which is kind of Eastern, has an average rent of $765; St. Louis, Missouri, $799; Philadelphia, $1,344.00; Baltimore, $1,700.00; Atlanta, $1,084.00; and Jacksonville, $1,009.20. *Yikes!* And New York is in the stratosphere.

Now a little averaging to compute those rents toward a $45-a-day factor based on the stretched 2006 collar:

Las Vegas	= $27.66 per day.
Seattle	= $34.16
Baltimore	= $56.66
Tucson	= $20.53
Albuquerque	= $22.20
Boise	= $25.53
Philadelphia	= $44.80
Atlanta	= $36.00
Miami	= $33.33

It's easy to see why Boomers are staying or will stay where they are, living in a paid for home, or possibly moving to the West or Southwest, where it's warmer and cheaper.

Utility bills factored in have all the flavors and sizes of an ice cream shop, and all the colors of a mottled rainbow. Who can figure, because they are changing all the time (and for sure, not going lower), and dissimilar cities boast their own power sources, and each apartment unit has its unique heating and air conditioning system. It's a job for an IRS-type accountant to figure out.

But using a solid but uneducated-arbitrary factor, the utilities are in the vicinity of 30% of the rental cost, the daily averages look something like this for the cities listed with the utilities added in based on the stretched 2006 dollar:

Las Vegas	= $35.95 per day.
Seattle	= $44.40
Baltimore	= $73.65
Tucson	= $26.69
Albuquerque	= $28.86
Boise	= $33.19
Philadelphia	= $58.24
Atlanta	= $46.80
Miami	= $42.90

Now it becomes clearer, unfortunately, several cities have been eliminated from this issue. But looking at the positive side: in Las Vegas $9.05 is available for food AND entertainment each day; .60 cents in Seattle; $18.31 in Tucson; $11.81 in Boise; and 2 dollars and 10 cents in Miami. It is possible to live on this amount with a minimal amount of fun. It all depends on what you consider exciting.

Of course, the above only takes into consideration major cities and one person. There are small towns and suburbs that offer lower costs and are just as much, if not more, fun. If there are two of you, you will have to spat over the fun-filled difference: fishing or dancing. There are several other solutions. The most obvious is to save money ahead of time, or maybe, rob a bank, win a Lottery, or have a lot of rich relatives.

If not, apply for a library card and read a bunch of books.

? On the road, before freeways were invented and cemented, we used to see these ... What were the Friendly Signs? And what did they say?

Stolen Identity

(Or: Who am I today?)

We all have said it at one time or another, 'I used to be somebody'. It frequently comes to pass after you've been finger walking through your high school year book; admiring your picture pushing a pair of black horn-rimmed or butterfly glasses through a camera lens. You look into a mirror and scream, 'somebody has pilfered my fine hair and replaced it with wrinkles and god-awful crow's feet creases on my face.'

About that time you'd gladly swap your SSN, credit cards, bank account and your SUV just to get your body back.

You may be, about that time, going through an identity crisis. Not the kind when you believe you are Gloria Swanson or Catfish Hunter, but when you think you are still in your teens or twenties. In fact, you know you are 18 because you can remember your hall-locker combination, you just can't remember if the school is still there.

It's not an amusing matter, but let's face it, some people should have their identity stolen to maintain worldly social peace, and you know who you are: You, the guy who comes to the party dressed in shorts and a shirt the same color as a penny jawbreaker candy machine, who drinks all the beer and makes moves on all the wives; the gal who wears a sweat suit that looks like its been laundered in plum sauce and Double Mint Gum, who purrs around all the available men.

Yet, when you get right down to it, identity merely is, after all, only a bunch of words used in the world of social sciences for an individual's comprehension of him- or her-self as a discrete, separate entity ... you. And in the world of finance it is all the personal info that can be used to drain your life of cash. The question comes down to: which is more important; social fair play or financial stability?

Protecting the latter is has a direct effect on comfortably continuing the former. Your ID must be protected from being stolen, and there have been a number of suggestions for protection thrown out by major organizations from AARP, to credit card companies, possibly the NFL, and maybe MAD Magazine.

Of course, there are outrageous proposals for protecting your identity, or at least not misplacing it; one is to tattoo your SSN on some part of your body. If one day you notice the number has changed, then somebody has swapped bodies with you and is out spending your money in Aruba. An easier method is to tape a photo of yourself next to the bathroom mirror, if one morning the photo doesn't match the reflection, either someone has snatched your wonderful body, or you haven't been hitting the exercise/diet program as much as necessary.

But getting back to earth, ID protections, especially your SSN, are keys you must turn in your brain once in a while. Your SSN is the key that unlocks all the credit information any body swapper would need. While shopping, don't carry your SS Card or anything with that number in your purse or wallet.

Avoid scammers on the phone and Internet and don't give information to anyone if **they** contact **you**. Shred all your personal financial trash, especially those free offers for credit cards and those blank checks credit companies mail to pay your bills; a dumpster diver can take them from the trash and cash them. Check your bills to assure the charges are only yours. And periodically check your credit report by calling 1-877-322-8228, or try online at https://www.annualcreditreport.com/cra/index.jsp for a free credit report.

Preventing your identity from being stolen today won't get you your hair back or make you younger, but will avoid you being taken to the cleaners tomorrow.

Seventh Sense of Seniors

(SPAM rhymes with SCAM)

That seventh sense developed by seniors over years of breathing on this planet has to occasionally perk up its ears and become alert to the whish sound of funds easing out of their bank accounts. Remember, SPAM rhymes with SCAM, and they both can be scraped from the bottom of your shoe. 9 out of 10 e-mails are SPAMMING and that's a lot of useless dung bytes.

After a few years of unconscious application, most seniors have mastered the 24/7 expertise of the 5 ordinary senses: <u>Hearing</u> only what is agreeable and understood, and screening out the latest Rock & Roll blast/rap attack; <u>seeing</u> everything while wearing glasses, but nothing when it looks like an in-law invader; <u>tasting</u> only the bitter and not the sweet and yummy; <u>smelling</u> only the sweaty feet and not the perfumed torso; and <u>feeling</u> a headache and hot flashes too often, and chills in the winter. All these are the routine operations robotically delegated to every-day senses.

Occasionally the Sixth Sense pops up like a jack-in-the-box poke in the eye of a common-sense routine to make life more interesting – ESP – that Extra Sensory Perception ... a power of perception seemingly beyond and independent of the well practiced and often controlled, yet tired and run down, 24/anytime, five senses. It's the mysterious intuition and the power that breaks into the daily routine to detect the exact nature of a person or situation.

Liar! Liar! You just know when someone isn't telling the truth. Danger! Danger! Impending danger is sensed and raises the hair antennas on the back of your neck and you fondle the pepper spray in your pocket. ESP, it has been said, also sends out mental waves to others across the world. "Call me," flashes through the picture show in your head, and then the phone rings. Coincidence! Who knows? You answer the door before there is a knock. Who knows?

But then again, it might be said, seniors just grasp the inner nature of things intuitively based on years of practice and experience: Exactly when to put the toilet seat down and not; And the radar that throws out screaming blips to avoid the guy in the flowery shirt and shorts at the Christmas Party. These are sorta the senior's Seventh Sense that only happens because of maturity, like the fine aroma of aged wine, the older the more it is finely tuned. We're getting closer to being able to read minds.

What is this Seventh Sense, then? You've been there before. It's not unlike talking to your self. It exposes daily episodes that come from years of experience and misfortune and are imbedded deep inside somewhere. Things like: Not acting without thinking; knowing when to keep your mouth shut; and not shooting off fireworks in the house. Some might call these instincts or common sense, but other may call it good or bad luck ... or timing ... or even learning by the adage, 'once burned; twice learned.'

Then occasionally appears the aesthetic level of the Seventh Sense. Like, how do you know a painting is good or bad? What brings tears to your eyes at a movie called Old Shep. It has sort of a bag-of-cats collection of emotions and paranormal entities that puzzle even the most realistic naysayer.

But does the essential Seventh Sense raise red flags in your brain and alert you of the approaching, sleazy mutt who wants your money ... all of it? With all your instincts and experience, it should. Your money can disappear with the flick of a mouse click. Your house can disappear with your signature on the bottom of the wrong document. Scammers can come dressed in any clothes besides a wolf's; unfortunately, even the clad rags of a sincerely concerned relative. "... money is twice tainted: taint yours and taint mine." Mark Twain is only about half right on this, money taint theirs, but tis yours.

Scams fall under many categories: Prizes and Lotteries where you get a letter asking for a fee to access your winnings; Psychics who will predict the winning lottery numbers and offer them for a price; Advanced Fee Frauds where scammers offer to share a large sum of money if ONLY you will allow them to transfer money from their homeland to your bank account; Pyramid Schemes; Investment Scams; Telemarketing fast talkers; and the list goes on. There is a web site put out by the Consumer Protection Agency supplies information on many of these damn spammers and scammers:

http://www.docep.wa.gov.au/consumerprotection/ScamNet/default.html

The latest attempt to drain you of your assets is the Home Refinancing frauds who say they can get you out of those high house payments with elevated interest if you just sign here. If you must do that, rely on your instincts and Seventh Sense and contact someone you trust, like your banker or the credit union. They can and will help. Remember the words from Bob Dylan, 'Money doesn't talk, it swears." But swearing after the fact never helps.

Third: Your Time Well Spent

Free Time is what retirement is mostly about. How time is used can be wasted waiting for the other shoe to drop, or spent in positive activities. You can *Go Fish*, or try pursuing another thing besides wiggly fishes, try *Hunting the Elusive Hobby*. This alone can be an entertaining project. But there are the usual suggestions, like *Bike Riding at your Own Risk; Bowling for Hollers*; or *Breaking Glass, Playing in Mud, Beating up Metal*. These are fun things to do; safe and exhilarating activities for changing your lifestyle and expanding you vocabulary as well as your wardrobe.

If you really want to waste you time and go insane at the same time, try golf, but, *Close Isn't Good Enough*. And then ... and then ... getting physically in top form at the drop of an ointment bottle by joining the *Gym Dandy Fitness Farm*. Then you will ask the perplexing and muscle aching question; *Getting in Shape is Fun, Why?* But all in all, you are having *The Time of Your Life*.

Go Fish

(Seniors can become kids again)

Warm weather comes along and some seniors opt to sit around and play cards. Others don't. Some may want to learn how to get wet and catch fish and become involved in all the rituals and debasing situations it puts them in. Why do it? It has been said, half the fun of fishing is just relaxing outside on or near the water.

Of course, the other half is maybe catching a fish. If there were a third half of the fun and an encouraging reason to do it, it would probably be a great opportunity to join friends in telling fish stories. And anyhow, what's the difference between being laid back in a lounge chair in front of the boob tube, or laid back somewhere pleasant with a line in the water? It's worth an examination.

For starters, don't be put off by tackle shops full of incomprehensible equipment or the misgivings that you can handle all the baiting, casting and hook removal with the proper gear. A tackle box the size of a Buick filled with wondrous and magic objects is not needed ... so they say ... but will come when you start to suspect the fish are smarter than you. A simple rod, reel, line, hook, bobber, some worms, and a six-pack will suffice to go fishing: You know, just like when you were a kid and dipped a hook and line dangling from a broom handle into the local creek. It's easier than it looks. Probably the best approach is to stop the time machine, become a kid again, and make it your whole new world.

Then you must consider there is fishing, and there is FISHING. So what method will you use, and for what kind of fish, and where? These are important questions to deal with. It looks so easy on TV. There's the guy wading in the middle of a river snapping his rod and line and fly across the water like graceful painter; the Huckleberry-Finn-type kid seated on the end of a pier with his line just hanging down while he's eating his sandwich; a well-tanned and macho chap positioned at the rear of a large craft with his line splitting the ocean in the boat's wake; and the cool cat leaning back in a small boat in the middle of a lake or bay with his line following any current that occurs. Which one will be you?

This is where geography and economics factor into your fishy decisions: Salt water or freshwater? How far do you want to travel? Is this a once-in-while hobby or are you building an alter ego? Do you want to fish every-other weekend, 100-days a year, or every day? What kind of fish do you like to eat (assuming you bring home the keepers)? Do you even like to eat fish? Are crappies worth the trip? Can your freezer hold a marlin? Are there enough catfish recipes in the world? Will others in your household put up with the live butter worms or smelly bait you're storing for future use?

If the mystery and seduction of the oldest woman in the world, Mother Nature, doesn't drag you to the old fishing-hole wonderland, then the poetic and vibrant names of the lures, spoons and flies may do it: Twitchin' rap, deep tail dancer, skitter pop and skitter walk, glass fat, pearl redhead, buck-a-boo, tiger tubes, flirty girty, black gnat, and so on. These are names that will stick to you like a fishhook caught in your collar.

The fishing rod has one quality it won't fall under: short. They are long poles that must be strong enough to pull in the biggun'. They're made of split cane, high-modulus graphite, fiber carbon, titanium, fiberglass, and material so light you don't even know it's there. Reels come in styles for casting, flying, trolling, saltwater, and pulling your truck out of a ditch.

You don't even want to get into the names and descriptions of the fish in the world without first having an acute dedication to this project.

Of course, what would fishing be without a few secret tips and techniques? For that, you must turn to a handful of experts, and they can be found everywhere and under any rock while looking for worms. Ask any of your friends, they will know.

Special techniques must be learned, like, tying the fisherman's knot. How to bait a hook is an important thing to learn. They say, once you get past the slime and wriggling, the tricky part of baiting a hook is getting the worm to stay on. Good Luck! Knowing how to cast might be necessary. Everyone casts a bit differently so don't be too concerned about form. An over-the-shoulder cast is traditional, but a sidearm cast keeps the menacing hook farther from your face and the seat of your pants. The point of any cast is to get your bait where you want it ... near the hungry fish.

The last and most basic question that must be answered and implemented before this new venture, 'The thrill of the first catch,' is, 'how much do you want to spend on a rod & reel, on a boat, or boat and trailer?' Nothing is cheap except that broom handle and the fish tales.

? What costs about 23 cents per gallon?

Hunting the Elusive Hobby

(The pursuit of an auxiliary activity)

As a full-time professional and former wage earner with jam-packed family responsibilities, you sometimes may feel a creepy need to fill up the modest idle time you have with some kind of distracting activity. Just sitting around, it seems, and listening to the rust build up around you just doesn't seem to work. You possibly get anxious.

Something is wrong with having that idle time with nothing to do. You feel the work-ethic wasp must have early in life bitten you and it has been attached to your guilty conscience. And finally, one day, you understand the problem, and realize how to solve it: you must hunt for a hobby – but where to start?

Now we're not talking about hunting for the Old World falcon, an elegant bird of prey, or simply called a Hobby, an elusive bird that dines on insects and small birds, and sometimes dragonflies. We are talking about the pursuit of an auxiliary activity outside your occupation and family that you can be engaged in for simple relaxation.

Hobbies come in many shapes, forms and activities and to choose one you must delve into a NASA sized research project. The list of options is infinite and come in distinct different categories with all the properties of a can of worms. Some come under the category of *keeping idle hands, the devils workshop, busy and creative.* These hobbies would include for example, model building, painting with oil, acrylics, or water, carving in wood, stone or clay; needlepoint, jewelry making, and on and on.

Others can be categorized under *legs on the move* because you have to walk, ride, dance, or tramp. This category combines physical health with mental health. Not an entirely bad idea. And another category is *keeping the brain waving and lively.* This consists of activities like collecting anything, playing chess, electronic games, cards (say, poker or canasta), family tree building, gambling (say, craps or horses), reading, and yes, even writing.

To start this hunt the local hobby superstore is a bonanza of information and ideas. You stroll through the crisscrossing aisles and immediately your work synapse snap signals to your pleasure genes hidden deep inside your libido. The aroma of glue and the small, slicing tools hanging on the racks bring visions of a cluttered workbench.

You fall in love with everything and can envision your home beautified with the creations: Model airplanes flying from wires attached to the ceiling. Better yet, remote-controlled model airplanes screaming across the skies over the neighborhood schoolyard; boats floating in your bath tub and in the community pool, or just casually sailing across the fireplace mantle; or model cars from every age and every country covering every spare road and highway in your home.

... Wow! There's not enough time to do it all, but you will try ... you will try.

Unfortunately the rules and boundaries of a home will soon invade your fantasy. You need the kitchen for cooking, the dining room for eating, the bedroom for sleeping and dressing, the bathroom for other stuff, and the living room for entertaining (although you may allow a little space for one or two models). That leaves the closets. There is also a little room left in the basement and the attic. Reality strikes its first fatal blow to your dreams. Your planes crash, boats all sink, and the cars are stuck on a freeway someplace in your home. Your glue gums up the kitchen sink and you suddenly have small-tool cuts on your fingers.

You move on to the next category of options, which prove simpler. Dancing is immediately obliterated from the equation because you haven't danced since the high school hop and found your feet weren't connected to your brain, anyhow. Tramping the woods and camping seems like a pleasant pastime, but it is mostly done on weekends, when it doesn't rain, and mostly in the summer and in the mountains, a far drive away. What about the rest of the year, and week, you wonder.

Now walking is easy, but you do that anyhow, and you don't consider it a hobby, but a necessity. Gardening is good, and you'll leave it at that. Running is just walking faster. You may not want to do that.

Bike riding is another subject and one you can wrap your legs around. You've seen bikes being ridden everywhere, by every one of every age, and you are part of the '*everyone*' species. City, country, day, night, fast, slow, or stop for ice cream or chase the sunset, it is an extension of walking, only with wheels: It has it all. With 24 speeds, a crash helmet, water bottle, a neat little pack on your back rack and riding gloves like an Indy racecar driver, it all sounds great. You may move this hobby to the top of your list—especially after visiting the local bike shop and seeing all the models and colors and accessories. You should be in good enough shape, after all, you walk.

You figure in fairness to the *collection aficionados* you shouldn't dismiss this category altogether. There may be some fun here and definitely another method for passing the time, as well as meeting people of similar interests. The *other people* element is an important secondary benefit of getting involved in any hobby. Stamp or coin or comic book collecting, it seems, is something that should have been started in childhood and built itself into a passion, sort of like gambling, it can't happen overnight, you figure.

Collecting dolls eliminates about half of the retirees. Although collecting action figure dolls eliminates the other half. Antiques are nice. Collecting old cars is something you could really get into, but your garage is too small: About as small as your budget.

The choice is obvious. You have to combine two or more hobbies into one. Some options are immediately out. You couldn't bring together candle making and knot tying; or jewelry making and collecting action-hero toys (well, maybe not); stamp collecting and bowling don't seem to fit within your personality profile; and dodge ball and acting your age would never be a good mix ... although you'd like to try dodge ball, just once.

Bike riding and collecting something could be combined; throw in traveling and/or camping, take a few notes for writing, and a hobby could emerge. Reviewing the combinations is endless and could be a hobby in itself, but is best left to each individual's quirks. But Watch Out, if a medium-sized falcon mistakes you for lunch. You're hunting the wrong hobby.

? Who said, "Plunk your magic twanger, Froggy!!! ... And where?

Bike Riding At Your Own Risk

Bike riding is a day trip and a fun-filled and healthy exercise. The air wafting through your hair, or across your bare head, or helmet, as the case and local law may be, and the drone of bike wheels as you coax your old-bone legs for more speed and extra hill power. Your gloved hands tightly welded to the handle bars as you wriggle from here to there. The feeling and fear you sense in the self-survival control of your muscles and an unknown destination. It's the best of times.

But, oh yes, there are some knee-scrapping NO NOs that should be aired out at the beginning, especially if you ride in a city.

The elusive and constantly narrowing curbside bike paths along the city streets; the verbal and sign-language interaction with motorists, especially those imposing on your space with a right cross to make a free-right turn; your respect of traffic laws (or lack thereof); intervention by helmet police; car doors casually opening in front of you as you squeeze along the right side of the right lane; mud puddles along the curb; and asserting your right to the road with a 30-lb bike vs. a 30-ton truck. This is some of the hair-raising fun you can expect.

Don't tailgate behind a city bus unless diesel fumes are your eclectic taste for dizzy-spell city air. That's not fun. Don't kick back at the chasing canine trying to retrieve your leg for lunch. That's not fun if it attaches teeth into your pant leg or ankle bone.

However, there are ways to combat the biking traffic turmoil tragedy. A rear light blinking on your bike night and day, a reflective vest or a safety triangle on the back fender, also night and day, are a couple of subtle lifesavers. Choose wide or slow streets or even back streets on weekends and navigate the city by traversing through neighborhoods, the slower a car is going, the more time the driver has to take aim; and for you to react.

Get a mirror to check your rear, but don't use it to dab on your lip gloss or check your teeth while coasting down a hill. Don't hug the curb but allow yourself a little space in case you see a large monster in your mirror approaching without moving over far enough to avoid you, or when you see that mud-puddle abyss oozing from a drain in front of you so you can veer around it. Watch out for those narrow cracks in the road, or old RR or trolley tracks that can grab your front wheel and turn your bike ride into a rollercoaster ride over the handle bars to OW-OW land.

Oh yes, again, there are risk-free places to pedal and coast your two-wheel, 21-speed magical horse. Through a city park, tracing a river, canal, lake, ocean or creek side, along an old railroad track converted to recreational use, or even along an old, closed lumber road. These are called city greenways which are linear open spaces that link parks and communities and provide public access to green spaces or a waterfront. No cars allowed, but other bikers and countless pedestrians slowly stroll along and do create minimum hazards, as well as again those occasional snapping canines that streak from behind trees to play dodge-the-dog tag.

A bike rack on the car, a clean straight back-country road, a high sunny and a lot of energy and curiosity day. These are the ideals for a day trip in the country. But be forewarned, there's nothing more exasperating than being miles from cover when a rainsquall drenches you and your plans and tries to propel you from your bike ... carry a rain slicker.

Most of the safety rules and cautions for city driving apply. Autos and pickups are just as nasty and huge in the country air as they are in the city haze.

Mountain biking is another day-trip opportunity for the healthy, strong hearted and insane. It can be dangerous, so it should be approached carefully; like feeding a hippopotamus. Imagine a Beetle Bailey cartoon picture after the Sgt. Snorkel has finished verbally and physical chastising him for being the laziest Private in the army. That's what you could look like after challenging a mountainside. You must have the correct bike with sturdy tires that ride over sand, gravel and Mother Nature's roughest terrain. Careful planning is a must or you may appear on the 6 o'clock news as a lost person.

It can be fun, but remember you are a second-class citizen because bike taxes don't pave the roads or build the greenways, big machines do. Around 44,000 people die in car crashes in the U.S. each year and about 1 in 54 is a bicyclist. WATCH IT!

Bowling for Hollers

So you are thinking of taking up bowling to pass your at-leisure time and fabricate fun in the company of similar human beings. Be careful what you wish for. After all, another bowling season is approaching. No rainouts, time limits, or union/owner holdouts, 24/7 lanes, and leagues that qualify anyone, all ages and sizes, even you.

Bowling has been around longer than you or your former boss unless you set up pins in the Egyptian tombs about 7,000 years ago, or bowled with the Polynesian Islanders the last few centuries. Bowling, as a sport, like taxes, is here to stay, it seems. It became a very popular sport in New York City in the middle of the nineteenth century, 400 alleys, and like billiards, it was even considered semi-respectable at that time, (what were they thinking?) except for the heavy gambling ... which made it decline in respectability.

And believe it or not, a sport that seems so distinctly American and very secular really grew out of a 3rd century German religious ceremony, too complicated to go into here, and not the rites and rituals of the TV phenomenon, *Bowling for Dollars*.

Knowing bowling terminology is critical so you don't look too stupid at the lanes. They follow the rules of any sport; you have to be there. Frame, Spare, Strike and Gutter Ball are common terms that even Gilligan and the Skipper knew as they threw coconuts at ten bananas. Did you know you could have a Dutch 200 game? It's by rolling strike-spare-strike-spare the entire game you can score 200. It's kind of like being 2/3's perfect.

A Turkey isn't your bowling partner but it's scoring 3 Strikes in a row, and a Sleeper isn't your other bowling partner but that pin hiding behind another pin in a Spare. And Foul isn't your husband after he's eaten a Snack Bar Burrito, it's crossing that line in front of you as you deliver the ball. Cross it, and listen to the caterwauling. It's a No-No, and you score an F, both common terms to all games, including life.

To score Bowling, check with NASA because they copied the scoring system to track incoming meteorites and it is too complicated to go into here. It has something to do with ten points if you score a strike, then adding those points to each following strike or spare, and so on. It's easy if you throw 12 strikes in a row because that is a perfect game of 300. But how 12 frames with 10 pins becomes a score of 300 is a Chinese puzzle that separates a bowler from the common people.

Luckily for us, though, in this generation, the computer geeks of the coming age have automated it and your score is automatically shown on a monitor above your alley. You can see it, and so can everyone else. No more eraser marks on the scorecard. Some alleys even have a little light near the pins to remind you if you are launching the first or second ball, in case you forget.

Dressing way down is the key to fit in. The multi-color and clashing mismatches of garments are a must; words and logos on the shirts and outrageous socks are mandatory. Shoes can be rented. We all know the sizes of the shoes range from Tinkerbelle to Sasquatch, and the reeking steam rising from them probably comes from those used by the Pilgrims at Plymouth Rock or the 300 lb. football player from Little Rock. But don't worry, they are anti-germ sprayed and colorfully striped so you can tell the right from the left. Best purchase your own pair, if you plan to make this a habit/hobby/regular recreation, as well a ball bag, ball rag, wrist supports and puffballs.

Look at anything around you, at any fancy shirt or dress pattern, the moon or sun or planets, any artificially derived hallucination, and you will see the color and look of today's bowling balls. No more black globs roaring down the lanes, but sparkling, colorful flower-like spheres bashing into the pins. And to make it more enjoyable you could name your ball, and even the pins.

Finally you must get the rituals down. A proper holler is a binding rule. You must say, semi-loud, after scoring a strike, "Yes!" or "Take that!" or something similar, then slap the hands or knuckles of your partners and yank the towel from the hook and wipe the perspiration from your brow. You did take, after all, 3 steps and a hop to make your delivery. Bowling is not an aerobics sport. A good under-the-breath mumble is necessary after missing a Spare. It shows that you care.

That's it. Have fun. And remember, it's not how you play the game, it's how you look playing the game.

Breaking Glass; Playing in Mud; Beating up Metal

(Seniors as Artisans)

The methods and processes seniors can draw on to create pieces of hard art are as varied and ingenious as the people messing with them. Breaking glass, playing with mud and beating up metal objects represent some of the fun activities you can look forward to. We're talking BIG here and not needle point or jewelry making, though they are highly regarded crafts by several people.

We're talking about the art of altering and shaping the earth's natural elements. The choice of styles and final products are as varied as the elements themselves. Each element possesses picky-finicky properties that require specific treatment to bend, carve, mold, or position it.

Take Glass – senior artisan wannabes can produce their imaginative pieces by means of several equipment-demanding techniques. Glass tubes can be bent and filled with gas (preferably neon and not biological); liquid glass can be heated, twisted and blown into various shapes, such as vases, ashtrays, or chandeliers; sand and glass can be arranged in designs and heated in a hot-hot kiln; or pieces of cut or broken colored glass can be used to create designs and illustrations for windows and walls, more commonly called stained glass ... although few stains are actually used.

Most of these glass techniques need specific training and information, which is probably available at your local craft shop, a large work space, and plenty of band-aids.

Wood – chosen from a countless number of available trees on earth and the neighbor's yard, is whittled, carved, chiseled, sawed, planed, turned on a lathe, routed, sand blasted, drilled, ground, sometimes chain sawed, or several other acts of deformation. What Fun! Then it is sanded, burned, stained, painted, sealed, puttied, polished, waxed, sometimes accessorized with another elements such as metal, glass, or clay, and finished to the senior artisan's whim. And finally, it is glued, nailed, screwed, clamped, assembled, mounted, framed, or positioned into the final vision.

Clay – or wet dirt, or more commonly known as special mud, is an earthy material that is plastic when moist, fun to run your fingers through, but hard when fired. With it you can create bricks, tiles, and pottery. The clay is chosen from a wide selection of colors. The artisan throws clay on a spinning wheel, molds it by hand, trims it, then forms it into a vision inspired by years of lifestyle skills; casts it into a bowl, pot, wall hanging, one more ashtray, or forms it into tiles to make ceramics for that new shower wall or coffee table top; adds color, stains, chemicals, glaze, patterns, handles, metals, etc ... then fires it in that hot-hot kiln.

Metal – steel, tin, copper, bronze, aluminum, lead, and pewter are pound, ground, bent, twisted, trimmed, filed, hack sawed, welded, molded, cast, glued, buffed, polished, painted, rusted, oxidized, or flushed in acid. Gosh, more fun! The artisan can use these delicate techniques, often combined with one of the other craft techniques and materials, to create a range of visions, including, jewelry, framed art, wall sculptures, gates, furniture (indoor and lawn), figurines, door knobs, mosaics, wind chimes, mobiles, another ashtray, and the list goes on. Some people use old junk to create fabulous, and useless, yet beautiful, junk art.

Here it must be noted that there is a fine line between Hobby and Mental Illness. A hobby is an activity or interest pursued outside one's regular occupation, etc. Mental illness is any of various disorders characterized chiefly by abnormal behavior or an inability to function socially, etc. Sorta close: Both are lonely pursuits.

Other pliable elements you can play with: Fiber – baskets, tapestry and wall hangings, embroidery, quilts, clothing, accessories, but not ashtrays, created by weaving, looming, spinning, knitting, crocheting, dying, hand painting, and tie-dying; using cotton, silk, wool, linen, rayon, yarn, and maybe grass or reeds ... so many materials and methods, and so many results. Sand – can be blasted against any of the above metal, glass or wood to gouge out patterns. Air – infiltrated with any-color paint or dye, shot from a gun in the steady hands of a visionary, and aimed at a canvass, wall, T-shirt, vehicle, window, or any flat or round surface (but not an annoying friend) creates images that range from futuristic nightmares to present day nightmares.

These are just a few hints for starters. To be creative to the extreme requires creative tools. Off-the-shelf material and equipment can only carry the senior's imagination so far, and then ingenuity must develop new materials and tools to create the picture projected in the inner eye.

Why would you do any of this? Nobody has come up with a good rationale. But with so much time available, there are endless projects to pursue for fun. After all, as the much quoted Mark Twain said, *Work is a necessary evil to be avoided.*

Close Isn't Good Enough

(To Tee or not to Tee)

If you are a senior and new to the game ... or considering taking it up ... follow the bouncing ball. Golf is such an all-the-rage yet controversial pastime, the best we can do here is summarize and categorize information, quote the experts, and allow the ball to drop where it may. Just remember, before you proceed into this world, standing on a golf course doesn't make you a golfer any more than standing in a garage makes you a hotrod.

There are so many off-the-wall rules, antidotes, quotes, personal tales, techniques, training hints and philosophies, the only useful revelations may possibly come by stuffing them all into a ball washer and letting it spit them willy-nilly onto the green.

Some of the basic rules for domestic safety are: Never go golfing with your wife; never go golfing with your husband; because here we see the nubbin of an endless debate. But one realistic rule followed by most experienced golfers is: Never go golfing with your goldfish unless you take your SCUBA gear or you train it to retrieve your balls from the #%$&*^ pond. This reveals a sparkle of sanity in an insane distraction.

As one unknown duffer (hacker) said, "I've spent most of my life golfing... the rest I've just wasted." This goes a long way in describing the commitment and madness of humans to a hobby of following a small, white ball around the world ... no matter where it lies.

Now let's put golf in perspective and separate it from other activities. The most elegant and successful pursuer of this insanity, Tiger Woods, has broken it down a bit for us. "Hockey is a sport for white men. Basketball is a sport for black men. Golf is a sport for white men dressed like black pimps." And the bowler Don Carter, "One of the advantages bowling has over golf is that you seldom lose a bowling ball." He has a firm finger-hole grip on his game.

Honesty has a dubious existence in golf. We've all heard of, thought about, seen it, and maybe done it, kicked a ball from behind a tree or pile of cow dung to get an unimpeded shot at the flag. Arnold Palmer (of Arnie's Army) one of the greatest hackers of all time exposed why he and others are so successful. He is a great teacher of the tricks of the trade, "I have a tip that can take five strokes off anyone's golf game: it's called an eraser."

Many aficionados support the revelation that Golf is a lot of walking, broken up by disappointment and bad arithmetic ... and maybe a good eraser or creative caddy helps. "Isn't it fun to go out on the course and lie in the sun?" jibes Bob Hope.

The best advice before the first golf lesson: learn how to stand and to move like a pretzel. "Have you ever noticed what golf spells backwards?' asks Al Boliska, but do you know it also stands for God's Ol' Lunatic Fun. " The only time my prayers are never answered is on the golf course," observes Billy Graham.

Exercise, fun, socializing and entertainment are the overriding goals of golf ... with restrictions. "If you drink, don't drive. Don't even putt," said the well know expert, Dean Martin. "I play in the low 80s. If it's any hotter than that, I won't play," admitted Joe E. Lewis. Then there's the exercise. "Golf is golf. You hit the ball, you go find it. Then you hit it again," long time professional duffer, Lon Hinkle, simplifies the absurdity.

A golfer's diet besides eating crow and chewing on knuckles after a bad slice or hook; live on greens as much as possible.

There you have it. There are so many expert quotes and dehumanizing rules and reasons NOT to take up the sport, that you may be disheartened, but don't be. There are also many more reasons to fulfill this dream, such as ...

Senior Quote:

"Does eating count as a new hobby? I became a gym-rat to counteract those dreaded extra 10 lbs." ...

Lynda: Plantation, Florida

The Gym Dandy Fitness Farm

'Exercise is a good thing'. 'Exercise is a good thing'. Write this 50 times on a black board or on the back of your hand, or better yet, post it on your fridge door and read it every time you **don't** open the door to get that pint of chocolate-mint marshmallow ice cream.

You know, or you should remember, grade school kids have recess when they run, hop, and dodge for an hour; high schools have organized sports and compulsory PE; college student spend a great deal of time running after the opposite sex; adults play at golf; and seniors seem to be satisfied with lawn bowling and bridge. Do you see the sinking undertone here ... older means less. Maybe seniors should regress to playing tag and dodge ball for exercise?

Of course, there are more grown-up alternatives ... like walking, running, riding a bike, 12 oz. curls at the tavern, and even ... heaven forbid ... planting your body in a local gym, perhaps called Gym Dandy Fitness Farm or something like that, for a regular workout. You know what a gym is, and it is not Grinding Your Muscles ... or Generating Youth Machines ... well, maybe. It is an athletic facility equipped for sports or physical training, or normally called a gymnasium, or semi-seriously known as a medieval torture chamber for the 'out of shape', and 'elderly'.

4-way neck; pec fly; preacher curl; super pullover (not a sweater); vertical chest; hip extension; and trimline elliptical. This is not sci-fi terminology or even titles of Stephen King novels. It is the everyday lingo depiction of the equipment in a gym. Quite possibly designed by Steve Gerberich, the creator of moving-mechanical-marvels art, but it is not. "Life is divided up into the horrible and the miserable," said Woody Allen, and he may have been describing this equipment designed for healthy-life purposes.

Now, you may be thinking **I'm too old** to join a gym. Think again. You won't be alone. You won't look stupid; especially if you dress for the gym and not a night at the opera. Modern gyms are littered with not-getting-any-younger bodies trying to reverse the biological clock. About half of them are of this grouping. Of course, some are racing against a sun dial, and some are keeping pace with a digital alarm, even occasionally you'll find someone trying to dodge time at a microwave pace. But the key is to find your timeline and work with it. You can't reverse the clock, but you can mess with the gears.

However there are alternatives to strapping yourself into an iron and rubber contraption and letting it bend your body back to youth. Unadorned and mundane old walking is a good thing; it's easy and accessible to one and all: but there are rules.

If you walk with a partner, which is good motivator to get out and do it, **walk** a mile a minute and not **yak** it ... it wastes good oxygen and tires you faster. Stretch before and after the walk to alleviate pain and cool the body down. Increase your distance every day until you get to the longevity level of 10,000 steps per day. Vary your route to make it interesting. And don't forget to go. Make a schedule and keep it. Maybe you can advance to jogging. "The only reason I would take up jogging is so that I could hear heaving breathing again," says Erma Bombeck, something to aim for.

Water aerobic workouts at the gym are another option. They incorporate a variety of rhythmic body movements and dance steps performed in both in waist- to chest-deep water and last 40 to 50 minutes. In some classes, equipment such as kick boards and hand buoys may be used. Programs vary from basic to the advanced. Water aerobics are usually led by a fitness instructor and may be performed with or without music by the Beach Boys. Rules for this activity are simple: you must get wet, and you must not drown.

And again there are the old standby workouts like stationary bike riding to nowhere, aerobic dancing without a partner, and working with a Big Ball.

For those of you who have been participating in the couch-potato routines of weight management, there are a few ways to ease into this exercise thing. Cardio workouts can first start with the simple act of climbing a flight of stairs, or two if you have the energy, rest a minute, and climb them again; repeat at least 3 times at first and build to your comfort level.

Second, with a quart of milk, or beer, or your favorite beverage in each hand, do a repetition of shoulder presses (lifting the bottles over your head and holding them there for several seconds) and repeating, again, to your comfort level.

Third is to stretch out flat on the floor and stretch the arms and legs a few times as far as you can, then relax; then grab your leg by the calf and pull it back toward you and hold for about 30 seconds. That's it, but every day.

An even easier start up the ladder of exercise is to do your house cleaning chores every day: vacuuming, cleaning the attic, sweeping the driveway, cleaning the garage or work shop, and for a good walk, emptying your garbage way down the block into the Supermarket's dumpster.

Or, if all of these seem too hard or too much work to become or maintain your health, you can follow the advice of Mark Twain, "I have never taken any exercise except sleeping and resting." Pick your poison.

? In the 50's, Wham-O sold 25 million of these in two month?

Getting In Shape Is Fun ... Why?

As adult sized, full sized, and maybe one of those oversized OPALS (Older Persons with Active Life Styles) you are at a distinct disadvantage from the *get go* when it comes to keeping fit. Why? Check your flexibility and stamina and blood pressure ... probably nothing to laugh at there. No matter what you think, you are not 20 years old and mind over matter is out the window when you are jogging down the greenbelt along the river or around the lake. Over indulging in fits of fitness, too quickly, is a sober reality that can hit you like a midnight cramp in your calf muscle.

There are gazillions of getting-fit charts and profitable promises made by slickers on the Tube and in magazines. Fine! Some of them work, but most of them only develop the muscles you use to retrieve money from your wallet or purse that will be passed on to the slicker.

Below are 4 lists of 4 things each to stick in your wallet or purse next to the money you want to save. These lists tell you the reasons and ways to stay healthy, how to check you fitness, and why to even bother. Being fit means to be in good condition, unfit is the opposite. The next time you laugh at a person who is terribly out of shape, be sure you're no looking into a mirror.

4 Reasons to stay fit:

- To collect all your Social Security benefits and to challenge Medicare to the max.
- To live longer and run up your charge cards to leave your kids a lot of debt in payback for all the money you lent to them that wasn't paid back.
- To maintain the same clothes size you have to prevent a new wide-size budget.
- So in the afterlife you come back as a puppy and not a pickle.

4 Ways to stay fit:

- Put a duct-tape cover your food intake valve (mouth) 23 hours per day.
- When eating, chew each bite 47 to 53 times to combine exercise with your diet regimen.
- Don't eat any fat unless it's your own.
- Never eat more than you can lift.

4 Ways to check your fitness:

- Jump into a swimming pool and if you float, your have too much fat, and if you sink you'd better hope you have enough remaining muscle to swim to the surface.
- Hop up and down on your right foot for half an hour. If you don't hop into the afterlife, your stamina is fine, but now your right foot is larger than the left. Reverse the process for full-body balance.
- To check the brain muscle, add your age to your I.Q. score (if you don't know what it is, guess) then multiply this by your shoe size. Divide this answer into you Social Security Number and add your mail zip code to the end of the answer. Subtract you phone number including the area code. If you've completed all this you can read and analysis. Your brain is fine or as loony as a toon.
- Repeat the first three tests every year on the anniversary of your high school graduation ... if you didn't graduate, then on the day you married your first wife ... if not married, on the anniversary of the first time you forgot to ... what?

4 Reasons to even bother:

- If you plan on living forever, it might be nice to do it minus a chair on wheels or a wicker walking stick.
- So you can lose weight and be able to pack only enough food in your shopping cart to fit your slim budget.
- So the opposite sex won't walk the opposite way when they spot you.
- So it will help you see where you are going and be able to fit through the Pearly Gates when you get there ... unless you come back as a pickle.

Time of Your Life

(Or: Are you a tree or a potted plant?)

So what! Nothing else works, including you. So you sit in your Recliner Heaven all day sliding toward the next day and into another year older! So what? What else is there to do? You have oodles of time on your hands but so little moola, and a colorful imagination is beyond the mental budget. So, sorting socks by color and holes frequency has become your hobby. Maybe you've graduated from the sox derby to the annual holes-in-the ceiling inventory. It's something to do.

There's always the TV memory carnival. It goes like this: I've seen this program before, but I'll watch it again because there isn't anything else on. Too much of this activity (or inactivity) takes up the time of seniors. The side benefit to this activity, though, is you can eat chips and dip until you create a shadow that will block out daylight-saving time.

And anyway, you're thinking about joining the Car Counters Club and sit on the front porch, in a rocking chair of course, and keep a journal of the number and caliber of vehicles in the neighborhood. That would be a great public service.

There are so many time lapses and boring pitfalls seniors can plunge into. It's easy to do. You've worked hard all your life, probably since you were 10 when you chucked newspapers at doors, and now you don't, and don't even have to punch a clock. Work is a memory; but free time is now your greatest asset. "Half our life is spent trying to find something to do with the time we have rushed through life trying to save." Will Rogers; U.S. humorist, political commentator, and showman. He found things to do all his life.

Now let's look at this from another viewpoint. If you were a tree you'd be productive by growing moss on your north side. If you were a potted plant you'd be reaching for the ceiling, millimeter by millimeter, sucking water from a tin can as you bask in the sun filtered through a windowpane while you beautify the room. If you were a cat, you'd be doing exactly what you are doing now; eating, sleeping, and not caring a tax token (you remember those) about anything else. If you were tumbleweed, well ... you know.

Can you imagine yourself being a tree, a potted plant, or a cat? Isn't that fun? Added to the mix these days there are computer games – and that's enough said about that.

Having extra time is a positive feature in the retired way of things, if used properly. Yes, we know, but, it passes so slowly, and sometimes takes forever to come and go. Look at it this way, now you can take that monotonous time and pursue all those little things you've wanted to do but never had the moment.

Of course, it has to be inexpensive and non-strenuous. Did you ever want to draw, or write? Then pick of a pad and pencil. One 94-year-old mother sits at her dining room table and draws colorful pictures of birds, flowers, and trees. Then she just hands the pad to friends and visitors and sits back and watches their reactions. You can do it, too. Along these same lines, some people create their own greeting cards to mail out. What a thrill you can give friends at the other end.

Hobbies can also be non-demanding group activities. Games played at a senior center, or even just a group of friends spending an evening or afternoon once a week playing cards, scrabble, or monopoly in a living room, exchanging recipes (or for that matter cooking them together), or for the more adventurous, darts or pool at the local pub. You can include another activity, walking, to avoid unwelcome encounters with the local flatfoot.

Some seniors have made plant care a hobby. You know, growing the Amazon Jungle inside the house. Some have even expanded this to caring for the plants of their friends and neighbors when they go out of town. Others have expanded this even further into house sitting ... that is, staying at someone's house and caring for it while they are gone on a trip. Maybe they'll even throw in a couple of bucks for your TIME.

Now TIME can be called ticks, tempo, a clock, era, hours, infinity or aging. Or it can be called drab, dull, flat, tedious, zero, or boring. It's in reality an attitude because TIME doesn't have a personality. It really is just the relationship we have with any event to any other, as past, present, or future, to paraphrase Webster. But time can also be good, time can be bad, or it can be the TIME of you Life.

Senior Quote:

"The most surprisingly fun thing I have found out about retirement? That I don't have to answer to anyone about what I do!"

Sid: Tok, Alaska

Fourth: Special Times and Events

The 5th *of July*, or the day after wham bam bang and sizzle, is a day of talking and reminiscing with old friends. *The Semi-Perfect Gifts*, the wishing well you open for Christmas, is a special as well as stressing times. But then comes along the little events that make retirement and experience. There's the *Winter Willies* when you grip your shovel and stand in the walk, dressed in wool and two pair of socks, you have to face the snow. The experience *of Déjà vu Driving*, which opens the question *Oh, Am I Driving*? Then there is always the first time you adventure out for a fine dinner, by yourself, and run into the *Single Senior Show*.

The 5th of July Again

(Or the day after Wham Bam Bang and Sizzle)

Yes, the 4th is Wham Bam Bang and Sizzle Independence Day and it is packed to the horizon with picnics, parades and band concerts all over the place; with decorations of red, white, and blue stuck to everything. But the 5th is the first day of the next 364 where the practice of freedom is really celebrated. A day to mull over what went before, and what will be from now on; sort of like a day playing country-store checkers after a day of an international chess competition.

The fire crackers have cracked and the rocket red glare is no longer in the air where the odor of burnt sulfur hangs around like an irritable family member. The ground is carpeted with paper confetti scattered by the fireworks and parades. But remember, the 5th is also the birthday of P. T. Barnum, the self-proclaimed prince of humbug; the day the Salvation Army was formed; the Secret Service was started on this day; and in 1946 the first bikini was worn in public. I don't know if any of these events have a connection, but if so, let's celebrate again! And some of us do.

This day-after day has always had a special meaning to those in the slower lane. If the 4th of July conveniently falls on a Monday or Friday, it provides another glorious three-day weekend. But those of us in a not-working-every-day phase of life say, *"Who cares?"* Mondays and Fridays disappeared from the calendar a long time ago. We no longer have to suffer through Blue Mondays because it was the first visible benefit after the last day of work. A favorite question on Monday morning in the elevator use to be, 'is it Friday yet?' And the normal response was, 'the third best day of the week, after Saturday and Sunday.' ... and it still is. Many of us in the past took the 5th off of work with the plan in mind to gently recuperate from the 4th.

The 5th inescapably suffers as it is the day after the giant rotating backyard BBQs, this year your house and next year someone else's, with all the trimmings, all the friends and neighbors, and all the merriment mess. The day after everyone has contributed their favorite casserole, salad, snack and dip, or a suspicious glob of something in the middle of a platter surrounded by a concoction even more puzzling.

Some bring their favorite meat or fish to smoke and broil in the open air barbeques, and everyone tries to top everyone else in the taste department; which makes for a wonderful feast. Many even drag in their own portable barbeques and lawn chairs so there'll never be a shortage of hot-coal surfaces or cool-comfortable seats under the trees. Ice chests brimmed with cooled beverages and tasty snacks are lugged in and spread to convenient spots around the back yard; and even in the house for those odd bodies who desire to dodge the sun's rays.

Following the afternoon and early evening filled with food and beverages, as usual, a short parade is organized to march to and then re-gather at the high-ground point in a nearby park or well-located street corner. The fireworks show begins at the edge of darkness and provides a spectacle full of oooh and aaah highlights, and concludes with the eye and ear shattering flurry of fire in the sky. The day is done for most of the partiers after that, especially those with kids, but some will retreat back to the house and backyard. A few of the beverages hadn't been tapped, the kids are gone, and a poker game seems to break out in the kitchen. Conversations and cards are dealt and replayed, and rehashed and reshuffled; food is eaten until the platters are clean; and one-by-one the players retire to the living room as the game diminishes down to a couple of winners.

And the celebration of the 5th of July begins a slow crawl to life.

"Remember when ... Remember where we used to ... Remember the time ... Do you know ... Can you recall ... Do you think we'll ever?" The warm radiance of the slight beverage buzz, or it could be the ambiance of old friends recalling memories, fills the room along with the morning sun and the flies seeking leftovers. Old friends who hadn't gathered for a while, for some of them a year, take the weight off their feet and relax in a comfort zone built by years of experiences together, and slow down. The distractions of the present are left at the door like dirty boots.

Someone always brings up the issue of those who aren't here this year. So-and-so has made a break for it and escaped south to warmer weather and the stories of *"I wish I could ..." and 'Maybe I'll ..."* begin to be fictionalized and exaggerated. Another soul mate has passed to the other side since last year and a rousing toast of beer bottles clang in a ring around the group, and an equaling rousing round of memorial stories bend the ears. *"Remember the time when we all hopped that freight car and ..."* and on and on the conversations spin, like a great habit: A déjà vu day that really has happened before and will happen again.

Yes, the 4th ignited the roasting fire, but the 5th maintains the warmth of the celebration. It is one of those rare days, year after year, when old friends gather and randomly reminisce. It is an annual day-after day, sort of like the 26th of December and the 2nd of January and the Tuesdays after Labor and Memorial Days.

The Semi-Perfect Gift

(The wishing well is open)

A Lionel Electric Train Set or a Barbie Doll: Most of us are beyond that elevated-expectations stage when we looked forward to and wished to find these under the tree. Even a Red Ryder BB Gun is out of the picture, apart from for those few who want that practical toy to confront an annoying neighborhood animal, from any species.

Candy cigarettes long ago have been replaced by the real thing, and recently abandoned as a social and medical no-no. Butch Wax followed the lost hair, and dolls have been replaced by the real thing. A gift certificate to the local Five and Dime Store is completely out of the question. Gosh, please not another tie or purse, 'don't need no more!'

No, there are almost certainly more appealing items on our wish lists these days: Probably more sensible things, like eternal youth, a more tolerant digestive tract, an un-trick knee, or even an entire stand-in body.

But modern science has its limitations, yet offers an abundance of constructive, if not rehabilitating, information. Remember that BAD coffee that should be sipped and not inhaled; now it has been exposed to possess health benefits, and even save lives. A few cups a day can reduce heart disease, protect the liver, lower the risk of type 2

Diabetes, and make us less likely to develop Parkinson's. Maybe even cure the hiccups: Who knows. Here we see the perfect gift as a lifetime pre-paid coupon for coffee at Starbucks. Can we picture a coffee shop as a health clinic?

Open the wishing well wide. We've all at one time or another wanted to midnight rendezvous with a movie star. In the old days probably Marilyn, Clark, or whoever was starring in the current Tarzan movie. But these days there are magazine and tabloid quantities of lovely and handsome stars to choose from for that semi-perfect gift evening, if only in our dreams. But in reality, to keep up with this gift, we'd doubtless have to drink a lot of that coffee. Science isn't much help here. Maybe a subscription to a magazine might fit the bill and save a life.

A chauffeur would be a great gift idea for saving time and sometimes health and property. The feel of a powerful engine wrapped with a luxurious body brings out all kinds of semi-perfect-gift and exotic emotions; taking us anywhere, anytime, anyplace. Hmmmm! But don't get those high expectations revved up because a year's pass to ride the bus will more likely be under the tree.

Of course, it should be made clear that each of us has singular wants and needs. If someone is sitting in the sun then she probably wants some shade; if up a river without a paddle, then he probably needs a lifejacket. Neither is a gift, but each makes life a little easier ... or longer. One person's gift is another's necessity. Take it further, those flashy specks and chunks used for accessorizing the body; are they really a necessity ... or a fuzzy-feeling luxury? Depends on the way we look at it; we can hock a rock but not a fuzzy feeling.

Or maybe the gift of mind reading, or x-ray vision, or the ability to fly, or super strength to lift the Sunday paper off the porch would be nice as well as practical. Well, in that case, we can hope to be transformed into a comic book character. At least we will lose some weight.

Possibly the best semi-perfect gift could be a mix; loading our stand-in body into a chauffeur driven limo and being transported to a Starbucks coffee shop to cash in the coupons with a hunk or a starlet decorating the table. To make it the just-what-the-doctor-ordered gift, the trick knee will not collapse while walking to the table. Aren't dreams wonderful?

Best ideas, keep the expectations low and practice the what-a-nice-gift smile used last year: Or hint ... hint ... hint.

? A fiery horse with the speed of light, a cloud of dust and a hearty hi-yo ...! ... Describes who?

Winter Willies

Winter is coming! Winter is coming! Grip your shovels and stand in the walks, dress in wool and two pair of socks, we have to face the snow. Weather is the arch-enemy of seniors and the whole world knows it. TV weather warnings in northern cities warn seniors to stay inside when the temperature plummets below zero or the wind hits 50. When we were 6, we ran for the door.

Snow – plows, drifts, shovels, chains, and tires materialize; ice on the windshield, in the carburetor and on the roads; frozen pipes; and icicles on the eaves and ears of frozen faces. No more picnics, no more parks, no more brisk morning walks ... unless in the dark ... with wind chill, numb fingers, and an everblasting runny nose.

It's time to modify your medicine cabinet for all seasons from sun-lotion land to VapoRub territory with an aspirin or two thrown in.

And your twice-over wardrobe?: A closet full of footwear from thongs to waterproof boots; a hall coat rack displaying flimsy to suffocating outer protection, hats and stocking caps, Norwester rain hats and sun visors and ball caps spinning around the top; and an accompanying once-in-a-while used umbrella stand. This seasonal clothing hits the budget hard. Cha Ching goes the old register.

"I was just thinking, if it is really religion with these nudist colonies, they sure must turn atheists in the wintertime," pondered Will Rogers.

Deal with it, you say? Of course, there are the snow birds: Seniors from Canada or the Northern or Midwestern United States who spend a portion of the winter in the Sunbelt region of the U.S and move back north in the summer. They move their warm-weather wardrobe back and forth. Cha Ching. Maybe the cost of a winter wardrobe COULD pay for a summer home in that warm zone.

There are simple but sober rules for seniors issued by most municipalities, the same as for Boys Scouts, *Be Prepared*:

- Avoid the icy patches on the sidewalks and long exposures to the cold
- Take breaks while shoveling the flakes (snow not neighbors) from the driveway
- Stay off the street and stay on your feet
- Keep your coat buttoned, and your gloves and hat on
- Don't get wet
- Don't drink too much alcohol
- Drink a lot of water
- Don't fall down and hurt yourself

The same things Mom used to shout at you as a kid when you left the house ... except maybe the alcohol part. Things don't change, they just age. "Every mile is two in winter," said George Herbert the medieval poet.

When exposed to the wintry chill seniors are at increased risk of hypothermia, a potentially life-threatening state in which core body temperature falls below 95°F. Symptoms include: confusion or mental disorientation; fatigue and irregular heartbeat. Additional symptoms may include shivering, slurred speech, memory loss, sleepiness, cool or pale skin, slightly blue lips or numbness in the hands and feet. So what's to worry? It describes your commonplace hangover.

We celebrate most major holidays in the fall and winter because they can mostly be celebrated inside. But when you must go out ... be as wary as a VW Bug in a NASCAR race. Put on those heavy treaded boots, grab that icy handrail or the nearest young kid, and avoid stairs leading to hell or a broken bone.

Victor Hugo said, "Winter is on my head, but eternal spring is in my heart." Words to have fun by as you slosh, not spring, through the winter.

Deja Vu Driving

(Haunting Habits Happen)

There are times when I really must do things different than I did for so many years. But things happen. Recently my Chevy took over my life and dictated my destination. Have you ever had that happen?

I was heading home from an insignificant event, coupon shopping at a supermarket down the road, when it happened. I wanted to make a left at the next light to shop at another market that had wonderful savings on vitamins and tissues: A cheap price and it was the last day of the sale. My car ignored the left and continued on until it turned right into my driveway. I'd missed the turn, missed the sale, and didn't realize it until I started taking bags out of the back seat.

What happened? I scratched my head, which I know solves all my problems, and realized that that was the route I drove home every workday for years. My Chevy was on auto-mode into that old routine. It drove home on its own. Like a faithful horse, it had that feeling it had been here before and out of habit followed the beaten path. Some call it sort of an eerie Déjà vu phenomenon. I call it a habit not broken. My Chevy just didn't know any better. Notice, I don't blame my memory, I blame the whole thing on the car. I also blame the Déjà vu God of Order in Life who is as overpowering and as intrusive as cheap cologne.

I'm all for order. It can be a good thing sometimes, like if I'm looking for matched sox in the dresser drawer, but enough is enough. For example, I finally realized a while back that I no longer must set an alarm because of the habitual pattern and many years of waking up at

6am; I still do, no matter how hard I try to sleep in. It is a routine I cannot break. I eat lunch at the same time every day, hungry or not. The remote appears in my hand and TV news goes on the same time every evening.

The experience of being under the control the Déjà vu God of Order in Life usually is accompanied by a compelling sense of familiarity (read boredom) and a sense of eeriness or strangeness. This I know from personal practice. I found through research that the previous experience is most frequently attributed to a dream, although in my case there is a firm sense that the experience genuinely happened in the past. My work history proves this last point. The only thing missing is my cubicle and desk. I do not want to be here. Do you know what I mean?

I also found that these haunting habits are not just created through work-related patterns; they can spring from any repetitive action. A friend of mine owned a cat for years and each evening before bedtime brought it in from the wilds of the back yard to sleep in the warm house. After the cat jumped through its ninth life cycle by unsuccessfully challenging a wild raccoon, my friend still hopefully ambled to the door before bedtime, opened it, and looked around. 'Just checking for burglars,' she would justify. In the corner of the kitchen there still sat the lonely clean food bowl and a sand box. Visual habits, a place for everything and everything in its place, are just as hard to break. I still trip over the ottoman that was there before the invention of the recliner.

Then there is the haunting habit that never happens. Another friend spent workdays in a bank data-processing department. Her job was to put out the fire if a system or cash machine crashed. She anxiously waited but never broke into an intense work mode unless reacting to a crisis; then she went into full throttle speed to solve the problem. Since retiring she is still anxiously waiting, and waiting, but not reacting because the problems aren't there: A habit not happening. Is this good or is this bad?

Not all habits are as bad as smoking: Like brushing my teeth; washing my hands after a workout at the gym; and eating soup with a spoon and not a fork. But I want to change and have that soup for lunch at 2:00 and maybe drive to a market too far. Better yet, drive around the city until I'm lost then find my way home. The opposite of haunting habits, I find, must be memorable adventures.

A light bulb lit up over my head. Small sojourns into the world of the unknown around the city are what will make this retirement thing a little easier to cope with. Big adventures such as trips to Maui and the Grand Canyon are nice, and costly, but the little book store or small café across town once in a while can make the day: The road unknown and the parkway to somewhere else suddenly became inviting. It will take me a while to retrain my Chevy to seek the unfamiliar, but once I brush the Déjà vu voodoo dust off its steering wheel and take charge again, good things will happen. They've happened before haven't they?

Oh, Am I Driving?

(Or: When is a long time too, too long?)

Do other cars or people or cats seem to appear out of nowhere and don't stop before you do? Worse, are the brake and gas pedals getting further away and the steering wheel growing ... blocking your line of vision? Do other drivers frequently honk before you get a chance to honk first? Have you had accidents, even "fender benders" you don't remember having, or discover dents that mysteriously appear on your fenders over night? Do you get lost, even on roads you know; while leaving your own driveway?

Have family, friends, or even your doctor worried about your driving, and they don't mean across the golf course ... unless of course you are in an automobile? Then you also should worry.

If you answered YES to any of these questions, you should consider seriously whether or not you are a loose nut. If you answered NO to all these questions, double check the list as if it's your food and bar tab at the local plush-plush food castle.

It takes thousands of bolts to hold a car together, and one nut like you to scatter it over the highway, and most of the time you won't be the one hurt.

Driving is a privilege, a pleasure, precarious at any age, independence extraordinaire, and an unparalleled breakthrough for getting from point A to point B since the invention of walking, or even running ... but not very good as an aerobics activity ... unless you're pushing the car. In the bygone days it was the most comfortable way to take a date to the Drive-in Movie. These days, it is a fact, if you are on the freeway, best to be in a car.

Most of us have been driving for a long time, but along comes a haunting issue, a life-changing consideration, 'when is long *too* long, or *too too* long?' We all age differently, or so they say; which raises the questions, 'when should you hit the bricks with your clodhoppers or hop on a bus? Or 'what age should be the upper limit for driving?' So, how do you know if you should bring to an end to a lifetime driving experience? Several states have mandatory limitation regulations of one sort or another; annual tests after a certain age, and things like that.

But some people don't have to lose sleep over this predicament. For instance, if you are steering a piece of farm equipment across 40 flat acres, no need to fret about hitting your neighbor's bumper. If you are on a dodge-em car at the county fair, don't be troubled ... aim at that friend who owes you money. Golf carts on the golf course are OK. But, if you race cars for a living, maybe you should think about cutting back on the races ... unless you're Paul Newman.

You don't want to be the character in this punch line – 'Mildred, you just ran 3 red lights.' And she responds, 'Oh, am I driving?'

If you must hang on, plan to drive streets you know, limit the trips, steer clear of risky spots like ramps and left turns at busy intersections, allow extra time, and most of all don't forget to put on your glasses and keep them clean so you can see what you don't want to hit.

"It just goes to show yah, you never really learn to swear until you learn to drive", said an anonymous philosopher, probably while in rush hour traffic ... probably behind you.

? What year did the Edsel pass through the Golden Gates of misjudged marketing errors?

Single Senior Show

(Dinner out alone after the Wallflower Parade)

Eating fine food in a quality restaurant is a dream for all senior citizens who have worked a lifetime and earned it. So occasionally, you may have the urge to enjoy a top-notch meal while indulging a setting with tablecloths, linen napkins, and silver, not plastic, tableware, please. Eating it alone is the nightmare.

You see, it's like being the focus of attention while crossing a dining room, like a wallflower parade with a string of toilet paper stuck to the bottom of your shoe, trailing like a bridal train, and people gawking, or worse, averting their eyes so they don't display any impression of an I-know-you glance. That's what it feels like, sometimes, and being a single senior this lightning often strikes when you participate in a social occasion of any kind.

The most uncomfortable event, and probably the most frequent, is at a stylish restaurant. It inescapably begins when you approach your first adversary, the hostess, with mild apprehension, because the first embarrassment typically comes about when you say,

"One for dinner, non-smoking, please."

"Only one?" she asks.

"Yes, Please."

Then the exaggerated yanking of one menu from the rack, and a full body twist and flicking of her blond-as-a-french-fry hair, *"This way, please,"* and the parade begins.

You know the spotlight is on you and can feel the buzzing of gnats as they swarm, attracted by the nervous sweat rolling down your brow and back. Every eye in the place follows you; you are sure. *'Please get me to my table as quickly as you can,'* you probably and silently plead with the hostess from the paranoid caverns of your mind. Then, after weaving around every table and being fully displayed, you arrive at your table. *"A table for six, don't you have anything smaller?"* you appeal to the hostess. *"This is all we have, unless you want to take a table in the bar?"*

They always ask that. They always want singles to be with other singles in the bar, drinking, so maybe you, some day, will be couples and can become a full-table bigger-tip customer. *"No, thank you, this will be fine."* You want to explain to her that all bars smell like dirty ashtrays and carpets soaked with spilt cocktails, and that truly spoils the taste of the fine dinner you are about to put out a good hunk of change for.

"OK. Your waiter will be, Smiley, and will be right with you."

"Thank you."

Now the second embarrassing adversarial event takes place. Busboy Bill charges the table and meticulously, with the grandiose flair of a Las Vegas magician, salvages the clean place settings of the five friends and family who obviously must have snubbed your dinner invitation. One, two, three, etc., the napkins, silverware, water glasses and placemats are scooped up and paraded across the room to the little nook in the corner where waiters and busboys congregate to plan your social demise.

It happens. It must. These degrading rituals can't be an accident. It has to be a social behavior created by generations of service workers, or taught in Restaurant 101. Who knows?

"Can I bring you something to drink?" asks Smiley the waiter who has more teeth than stars, Busboy Bill's ally in torture.

"Just coffee."

"Just coffee?"

"With cream, please."

"Nothing from the bar?"

There it is again: the bar. *"No thank you."* From that time on the dinner goes just fine, except the eternity between when you've ordered the meal, and the point when the meal arrives. What to do? In a small diner or café, you usually would whip out the daily paper or a paperback and read it while sipping coffee. Here? No way. It would be like waving a red banner, **Lonely Person! Lonely Person!**

During the meal, the eating part of it, after it parades in dish by dish, you get the usual courtesy drop-bys from Smiley,

"More Coffee?"

"Everything OK?"

"Will there be anything else?"

Moreover, invariably on each of these occasional visits your mouth will be full of food and you must either nod your head or spray a mouthful of it across the table if you say *"More coffee, please"*. Again, they must also instruct waiters and waitresses how to do this with faultless timing at Restaurant 101. This is where universal sign language enters. You must point at the cup and nod, yes ... or no.

After the meal is complete you need, **must** obtain, the check so you can calculate the amount of a tip and escape through the front door. Smiley saunters past with 6 desserts somehow attached to all hands and arms and strides a beeline for a family at another large table. You move your plate away to signal that you are done.

Smiley brings a pot of coffee ... to another table; you need coffee, too, but don't get it. Finally, you place your napkin atop the fragments of food you've left on the plate, then nudge it to the edge of the table ... and wait.

Busboy Bill is more attentive and captures the plate, silver, cup, saucer, and water glass, and remaining are a couple of peas you'd accidentally brushed off your plate. The tiny peas somehow have become plugged into an electrical outlet and developed strobe-light characteristics, which are attracting the critical eyes of everyone in the area.

Smiley passes again. You try a casual wave: Once, Twice. Then you realize you must make a dash for it. You place enough cash and a proportionate amount of gratuity, undeserved you believe, on the table and attempt to sneak out around the happy diners, past the hostess, and toward the front door, hoping all the time you don't get stopped and accused of an act of **Dine and Dash**: All the time, of course, *dragging the same toilet paper train behind you that you dragged in.*

You retain and cherish its possession so you can display it at your next stop alone, the theater.

Fifth: A Better Life for You

? *is better than* **?**, means more fun. *A Second Lifespan,* just the facts Mam, or *A Second Heartbeat,* a new cuddle buddy or, in other words, a pet, would be good things, too. New clothes by *Dressing Down* from work clothes to play clothes, or adding to your scrap heap of personal memories by learning about the new world and expanding the *Noodles and Beans between your ears.* These all can lead to a better life.

Sometimes a new job is desired and *Help Wanted* situations are challenging, and *If You Must Work to Work to Have Fun,* let it be good. *Bad Hair Days,* better known as Murphy's Law, are always lurking there. But be sure that everything is always '*Cool*', and forget who *You usta be.* And *FREE, is it a Fixed Price or a Down Payment?* Beware of *The Enemies you Buy* and all those *Vital Statistics* that can catch you off guard.

? *is better than* ?

(Or: multiple choice meltdowns and true/false tremors)

Know what you are doing and where you are going in this new venture called the Boomer age ... even if you are a pre-Boomer. To do this, you must find out **what** is better than **what** for planning ahead to a fun-filled and easy-going existence. All your life you've been forced to make decisions for others. But now, being a Boomer-in-leisure, you probably feel you should be able to coast along without a care in the world. Not! After all, Prepared is better than Not!

First, there are some things you most likely know right off the get go: dark chocolate is better than tan; whole wheat is better than white bread; bran is better than sugar; fun is better than fear; hair is better than bald, naturally, but no choice here; gray is better than black, unless you're dyeing for this decision. Good health is better than bad or fair.

Men are better than women. Women are better than men. Compromise is better than a black eye. Sun is better than snow, except for you who have masochistic tendencies to strap wood to your feet and plow breakneck speed down a steep mountain. It is also an almost proven rumor that cold, damp weather and arthritis mix to make painful joints.

So many choices and splits in the road down retirement lane; so many decisions, multiple-choice meltdowns, and true/false tremors, and everyone said it would be easy.

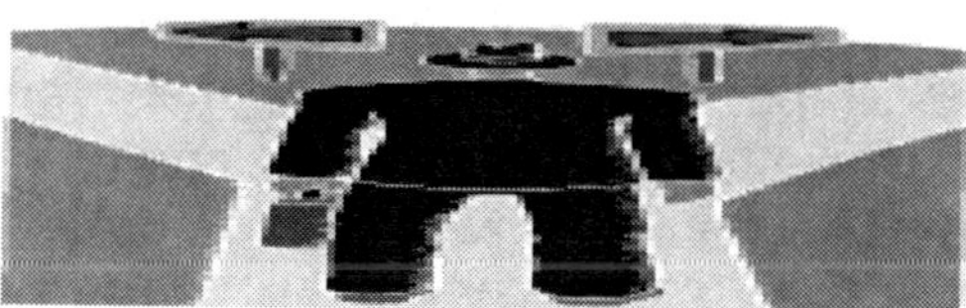

"It is better to keep your mouth closed and let people think you are a fool than to open it and remove all doubt," observed Mark Twain;

or, as many other people say, 'two heads are better than one, and a hundred are better than two' (unless you are feeding them). In other words, get help and advice with some of these important decisions. So get with it and decide your future. It's almost as important as your golf game or the Super Bowl.

Habitat decisions: Where to live? Sun is better than snow (see above) most any time, and swimming in water is better than spraying it on the same old lawn for the many years to come. A swimming pool is better than a motor pool. Too laid back is better than too busy. But moving locations is a major decision and you will encounter oodles of side roads, too much baggage, and mind-bending detours.

The first decision is, '**should** you move?' and then, if you do, what do you bring and what is left behind? What about all the 'packrat assets'? That is, all the stuff you've saved over a lifetime in a large house, and how to stuff this stuff into a small condo. You can't bring any of your friends or acquaintances, so you'll have to start over there. So, is moving better than staying?

A nest egg is better than egg on your face. This is an observation that should have been made a while back with a flock of financial friends funneling you through the matrix of percentage points and plans. But, it's never too late to enhance that egg with skillful saving and extra income. Some might come from selling some of those packrat assets for cold cash. How much is your house worth, and is that cash better in a bank or in the form of wood or bricks holding up those packrat assets.

Then the ultimate, important question arises, when to retire –

50, 62, 65, 70, or never?

Maybe only semi-retire, that is, collect all the retirement benefits, including SS (but be careful of income limits here) and work that part-time job or make your hobby finally pay off. This is where fun is better than work comes in. This is all a very personal decision process where, maybe, no one else knows the answer better than you. But one thing is certain, what's better for you is better than anything else.

And then there is the ultimate friend's or ally's destructive comparison, I'm better than you. Who cares?

Waffling, fence walking, hedging, changing one's mind, gray areas, uninformed choices will all set up roadblocks, but if you have the capacity to learn from mistakes, you'll learn a lot about yourself and what you want and who you want to be in the future by going through the process.

? "Rock Around the Clock"?

A Second Lifespan

Just the Facts, Mam

Being a further up the ladder ain't so bad. It's sorta like having a second lifespan. An informal government fantasy-fact-finding survey conducted in the backrooms of a Las Vegas casino determined that seniors are probably much older than most other humans, thus, they must be smarter, richer, taller, more-worldly people, and possess all the qualities of Superman and Wonder Woman. If you had to identify, in one word, the reason why the human race has not achieved its full potential, that word would be *meetings-like-that.*

The study was conducted by a multi-paneled group consisting of one member from each political cluster, fraternity/sorority, religious sect, social organization, and stag party. The 30-some-thousand panelists met by conference call in 30-some-thousand Starbucks coffee shops throughout the country. Interviews were conducted, recorded, analyzed, and edited; studies taken with diligent notes, plotted, graphed and printed; and the ominous facts were verified by Dick Gregory and Bob Newhart wannabes.

After the study was released, a reporter was interviewing a 104 year-old senior-senior lady playing the nickel slots: "And what do you think is the best thing about this study and being one of the top dogs at104?" the reporter asked.

She simply replied, "No peer pressure, but that's an old joke."

That may not be lock, stock and barrel true these days: Funny or not, in the 1990 census there were a total of 37,306 centenarians (somebody who has lived to tell the tales and lies past the age of a hundred), living in the United States—and 6,359 of them had celebrated their 105th birthday.

Then the reporter asked, "Did you get your letter from the President?" In the United States, centenarians traditionally receive a letter from the president upon reaching their 100th birthday, congratulating them for their longevity ... and in all probability asking them for their vote. Willard Scott of NBC's *Today* show has also named them on air since 1983. "Yes, she said, and he did ask for my vote, but I shot back a letter to him saying, 4 years is quite a long time for us senior seniors, so I'd rather vote for Willard."

Seniors being worldlier people might be closer to the truth. Travel is a top activity for seniors, and they spend more, travel more often, and go further than younger earthlings. And they rip up the highways with RVs and part the waves between the islands as cruise passengers more than anyone. And here's a shocker, they purchase more toys and luxury cars, and are online more than teenagers, thus they do a lot of shopping there. Richer might be a closer description than smarter, because they also spend more.

A subcommittee comprised of Texas Hold 'em Dealers, self professed experts on the bluff, found the Biggest Scam. While investigating deceptive sweepstakes practices, those companies that target seniors and make them think they will receive a bunch of money, but in reality they never see any of it, found the most deceptive and disparaging of these scams are called Social Security and Medicare. A sub-sub committee agreed this was 'horrible' and elected to pass this information under the table to a sub-sub-sub Senate Committee for further examination sometime this century. The word is, don't count on them for much help.

Considering retirement as a second lifespan is mostly and probably positive. Twenty to maybe forty years while starting out with a world of experience behind you instead of a diaper on your behind. That's a real head start ... so to speak. Retirement has so many options for doing little, and we should make the best of it with all the practice we've had. The key here is, you likely stopped celebrating your birthday at about age 11, start celebrating it again at 65.

Look around you. According to some, there could be as many as 850,000 centenarians by the year 2,050. As life expectancy continues to climb, more and more of us will span across centuries. It could be you. Are you ready for a second life? Are you active? Are you healthy?

Senior Quote:

"The most surprising thing about retirement is that it's a lot busier than I had anticipated. My dream retirement had me lying in a hammock with a Tanqueray Tonic and a cigar, watching the clouds roll by. For some reason, there always seems to be something that needs attention, maybe after we finally get settled into the new condo in Waikiki it will slow down a bit." ...

Audrey and Ralph: Honolulu, Hi

A Second Heartbeat

(A cuddle-buddy tale)

A crony recently advised me that I needed another heartbeat. I immediately threw my hand to my chest hoping for another ... and again another after that. 'But the doctor says I'm in great shape', I gasped. 'Not a transplant, idiot,' he put in plain words, 'a second heartbeat, a companion.'

Because I am a single senior and tired of eating TV dinners and take-out food my mind immediately flashed brilliant colors of Las Vegas ladies and gala parties, but I knew with all that going on I may need a third or fourth heartbeat to keep up the pace. 'A pet,' he clarified, 'a second heartbeat, a cuddle buddy, someone to talk to rather than your impassive walls.'

My walls do just hang there and hold up the pictures and doorways. My friend probably had a point. I had to give it some sober thought ... and thorough research ... so I started analyzing my way through the animal kingdom ... starting with the most common heartbeats ...dogs and cats.

For the most part dogs seem to be slow on the uptake, but loveable and active, and they come in a variety of sizes and colors. I figured *size* related directly to food consumption and dumption (if there is such a word to tolerably describe the process of following an animal down the street with a plastic bag in hand), and *color* related to shedding to match the carpet.

Cats are too mysterious and I am positive each one stares at me with the intention of trying to possess my human soul. That scares me. I have enough trouble keeping my soul pointed in the right direction without it being attached to a cat. But cats do have a lot of fun and are fun to watch, from a distance. They run around the neighborhood, unleashed, and chase birds and an array of imaginary wildlife they eyeball from an ancestral crouch.

But cats and dogs are old hat and everyone has one, I figured, so a visit to a local pet store might reveal a menagerie of other heartbeats.

Birds are colorful, small and easy to maintain and can chirp or chatter or sing. Canaries are petite and sociable, as long as you don't touch them (sounds like some people I know), and can live up to 25 years. 'Wait a minute,' I worried, 'I may have to include the canary in my will.' Macaws are beautiful, but large and they can live to the age of 50 ... another inheritor to my vast estate of packrat artifacts. And a plain old parrot, if taught to sing O Solo Mio like Enrico Caruso, will be a real pain in the brain in no time. Besides, where do you put a birdcage in a SUV while traveling across country?

Do snakes have heartbeat ... a heart? Does a fish have a personality?

When is the last time you had the opportunity to cuddle and pet a rat, or even escort one down the street on a leash? I was told a fancy rat, I supposed as opposed to a Cinderella-at-the-Ball rat, is an ideal pet for the ages 8 and up with adult supervision. (Being over 8 I didn't know who I could ask to supervise me in my pet play time.) They grow up to 10-inches long with up to an 8-inch tail. My O' My! That is a foot-and-a half of rodent fun and maybe I could escort mine on a leash down the street ... that is if I want to lose all my neighbors as friends and risk an attack by cats. 'You should have two rats', I was told, 'they are smart and can learn tricks ...but they have large front teeth and need something to chew on.' Between the tangled leashes and my gnawed finger stumps, I passed on the rat(s) as a second heartbeat.

Then there is the reptile family of pets. There is a variety of reptiles beyond the slithery snake group. How about a Crocodile Greco, a Panther Chameleon, a Blue-tongued Skink, or an Argentine Horned Pac Man Frog? All are genuine animals and not Sci-Fi creatures. And you know what? These pets eat live insects and worms that also must be fed nutrients before they are fed to the second heartbeat. I passed again.

While considering the second heartbeat I also reflected on some of the secondary responsibilities. Cleaning up after any second heartbeat will be an olfactory challenge no matter what the source: Cats are not clean animals – have you cleaned out a cat box lately? Little doggie-poop baggies are just disgusting. Stained and dirty newspaper bottoms and littered water that must be changed, and sweeping the floor of a reptile cage littered with insect carcasses could be downright memorable.

There are a few other outlandish things to consider, such as, a decent burial for my second heartbeat in a Pet Cemetery; before that Veterinarian expenses; related to that I recently read that I may have to send my second heartbeat to be consulted by a member of the IAABC (International Association of Animal Behavior Consultants). I saw a sign in a pet shop I was browsing that advertised 'Have your pet's photo taken with Santa'. Come On! But the one I read written on a bathroom wall made me feel a little queasy, 'Keep our city clean. Eat your dog!"

There you have it, and as a man of strict indecision and sticking to it, I decided my friend was right and decided on a pair of second heartbeats to keep me in high spirits: a spaniel puppy and a wirehair kitten.

Dressing Down

(Buying new rags for a retired body)

And I was positive I knew what I looked like in the mirror all these years. But, to say it wildly, the other oxford dropped when someone asked, “Do you know what you truly look like in those clothes? Are you comfortable? It’s a barbeque, man. Loosen up” I had to admit I’d ventured out on very few shopping expeditions for new rags since I embarked on my finer life of leisure. I began to feel like an eight ball at a beach ball party.

Someone then suggested I wear a brighter and more colorful shirt for a photo shoot. I can catch a hint. I figured I’d better examine my closet and I found it looked like a typical day in the Pacific Northwest; a dull assortment of grays, blacks, whites and occasional shades of blue ... my dress-up clothes for many years that served me perfectly well in the office/cubicle/boardroom world. The only traces of a rainbow in my closet were the neckties, which I pledged I would never knot to my neck again; at least I knew that much about casual wear. A light bulb lit up in my brain, wearing my old work clothes as party clothes wasn’t socially acceptable and a major fashion modification was not only in order, but socially necessary.

After that degrading comment about my casual rags, I scrutinized the attire of my friends at the party, men only, because women always have two or three floors of wardrobe to choose from at any department store, even their work clothes. Men's clothes usually hang along racks between the tools and the shoes.

I deduced that casual clothes for men materialize in three fundamental styles: The golfer motif, which depicts the impression that the displayer of this costume is arriving at or coming from the 18th or 19th hole; Hawaiian-loud designed attire says vacation is my game and I've been around and I don't want you to forget it; or then there's the racetrack bookie garb that falls between an imitation of Cary Grant and the used finery purchased from a pawn shop. Believe me; any combination of two of these styles creates chaos in the GQ world.

I decided it was time to dress down and I ventured into unknown territory to shop for my new rags; I wandered the streets of the city rather than the aisles of the clotheshorse arcade.

I stumbled on a store that specialized in sneakers where just about any creature from the animal kingdom or any barometric condition on the weather map could encase my feet: choosing from the basic activities of walking, running, cross training, basketball, skateboarding, casual or courting. Being a single guy I opted for the latter; it seemed like an all-purpose shoe with a sort-of-flat sole and a conservative gray color ... hard to kick the habit.

Working my way up the torso new pants was my next objective. I remember when jeans were simply called blue jeans and had the little watch pocket in the front and a leather label on the back under the belt. Now they are called denims, Levi's®, Wranglers®, and an assortment of cowboy (girl) descriptive action adjectives and fashion designer dialog. They carry descriptive styles like boot cut, pre-shrunk, cargo, carpenter, relaxed, easy fit, form fit, loose fit, straight leg (What? As opposed to a broken leg?), patch pocket, paint splatter, boomer (now if that means baby boomer, they might fit me), and adult cut; baggies were out because they dropped below my love handles.

I had to make a fundamental style decision, that is, do I want to look like an adult type person or a pre-shrunk-relaxed-easy fit type of casual person? I assumed the obvious and bought the adult style, which I quickly splattered with paint and dragged behind my SUV a few miles to make them look in style. Of course, there are alternative choices such as casual slacks, khakis, cords, and wash and wears, but I decided to hold off on buying any of those until I lose my extra weight at the gym.

I began to get into this fashion-plate mood and decided to venture up the body parts and cover my middle-aged spread around the breadbasket. Since I live in warm territory, and because the color of my jeans and sneakers were close in color to my work clothes, I decided on a clashing rainbow collection. There were polo, golf, tennis, and sport shirts; long and short sleeve; pocket and non-pocket; with or without a moose, alligator, brand name and golf club embroidered on the chest; multi-colored and plain; and one size larger than usual to cover all the good-time meals I'd eaten in my previous life.

Hats are a mood thing and my mood is usually not to wear one, unless it's raining too hard or the sun is shining too bright. I could hold off on jackets and sweats until the weather cooled to room temperature.

There, it was a plan; I bit the bullet and shopped till I dropped. I selected a set of sporty clothes that I'll wear to the next barbeque. It's a different approach than the three styles I'd observed on others. I looked into the mirror again and recognized that I am now a retired teenager: Next, a ponytail, tattoo, and pierced ear.

? Whose Father starred in Sea Hunt?

Noodles and Beans

(The scrapheap of personal knowledge)

Yeah! You've heard it all before: school, classes, learning, furthering your education. They suggest seniors take classes to stuff more information and memories into your already overtaxed brain. You did it for years and are thankful it's over. You sang it as you dangled your Hopalong Cassidy or Mickey Mouse Club lunch boxes from your arm and skipped home on the last day of school, the opening day of the rest of your life. '*No more school. No more books. No more teachers' dirty looks*' or something like that.

You cheerfully dumped that lunch box, got a job, got married and had kids, or went on to the self-determining lifestyle of college, or back-packed around Europe, or did nothing. No more rows of desks and cramming for a-waste-of-time test about the inners of a dissected frog for us. Why do you need more?

Yeah, you may say, in our day we saved the world from itself: changed its black & white mind-set to a tie-dye positive outlook; moved free love from the back seat to a under a tree in the park; filled the air with music mixed with smoke that climbed into everyday brains; and we may even have stopped a war or two ... isn't that enough. That was fun at the time and almost as cool as spitball fights and wedgies in grade school.

What more can you do? *"I read Shakespeare and the Bible, and I can shoot dice. That's what I call a liberal education."* Tallulah Bankhead said that. Did you understand what your grandkid or the kid next door just said to you the last time you chatted? They were talking in the present tense. Are you? Explain a byte or a RAM or rap. Maybe more is better.

There are so many memories, or retained personal knowledge, you've stored in your noodle salad of a brain in the center of your bean and there just isn't room for any more ... maybe.

Memory is just the process of recalling or reproducing what has been learned or experienced. Some believe that memory loss isn't as much memory loss as it is slow memory declassification and retrieval. You know the answer is there, it's just you have to rummage through years of living and experience to connect the dots to the question. It takes time to shuffle those dusty files and synapses, and the more storage piled up in the noodles, the slower the response.

But there is no end to the storage capacity of your personal bean, and with a little more time on your hands now you can store whatever knowledge you want. If you ever get tired of contemplating your toes from the lounge chair, did you ever wonder how paint miraculously takes shape on a canvass and creates an emotional image and a novel brings tears to your eyes? How do you shape clay into a believable likeness? Are you too old to learn to tango? Maybe take a chance to see if you can overload the bean.

You see, education doesn't have to be about projecting the collision of two planets several light years away and a million years from now; or reading poetry that you couldn't understand even if you read it hanging upside-down. "*There is much pleasure to be gained from useless knowledge*", said Bertrand Russell. Let's face it; most of what you know is useless knowledge anyhow. So, kill a little of that extra time, learn something new, exercise that memory muscle and add to your scrap heap of personal knowledge. What's the harm?

? Buckwheat, Alfalfa, Spanky, Darla and Petey were members *of* what notorious gang ... and when?

Help Wanted

(The supplementary income game)

Hat in hand, you must do it, that is, carry out the most multi-faceted and degrading action-reaction performances devised for humans since the beginning of the Industrial Age, that is, hunting for a job and the embarrassing, knuckle-gnawing interview. The unexpected is anticipated. Humility is the strongest asset you can bring to the table. You know that. You must be pleasant and have a silk suit and tie on your tongue with a button-down brain cluttered with pearly smiles and polished pleases if you want this extra cash.

The interview process, usually, in the past, in most cases, unfortunately, after the interviewer, typically a fresh very-young graduate in Human Resources from Matchbook Trade School, after glancing halfheartedly at your resume, seems to consist of two questions: 'Why do you want this job?' 'And, can you find the door?' Your gray hair trips you up every time.

While **waiting** –perspiring like a lawn sprinkler– in the **waiting** room before the interview, dwarfed by youth, vitality, and the latest fashionable outfits, reality hits you in the face like the bottom side of a frying pan. It must be a weighty enough task for a young person to apply for a job or plan a career in these days of high-speed mutation, but what about a senior and proven useful individual? You just want a meager supplemental income to keep the corporate collectors from busting through your door, while at the same time doing something with your idle time. You squirm in a folding chair in the waiting room and feel like a no-nonsense tennis shoe at the Governor's Ball as the tasseled loafers pass you by.

Remember what President Clinton so eloquently announced to an audience a few years ago, "By the time our young people reach your age, they will be working jobs that haven't been invented yet." Great! You see so many young people around you who have fingered through the yellow pages shopping for the Acme Futuristic Trade School. They are hoping to master those yet-to-be invented jobs, or have applied at a local community college and asked, "Can you enroll me in all the classes for a job that doesn't exist right now, but will pay me those 'big bucks' twenty years from now. And by the way, I'll take my $1500 tax credit in cash." They are at least smart enough to know that whatever they learn today will be obsolete tomorrow because technology is moving too fast. You feel their distress. You didn't know the Pres. was also talking about you.

"What about me?" You shout from inside to the indifferent world around you. "I'm available, a neat dresser, experienced, and actively in the job hunt," but all you have found, though, are openings for trained and proven senior professionals that range from a Superstore Greeter to a Café Swamper. You guess they have determined any older individual can shake a hand, swing a mop, or drive a delivery van. If all else fails, you may have to resort back to delivering the morning newspaper like you did when you were 10.

Despite all you must continue playing the game. Two dailies thumping your door: Opportunity knocking? Wonderful! *Men Wanted. Man Wanted For*. Circle and call. Circle and call. You do the expected classified routine. They always say the same things, "Not today, sorry! All filled up today. Call again tomorrow or after you reincarnate as a younger version and own a bigger car." You can't demand. Your resume and applications are probably stashed in file drawers all over town between chopped olive sandwiches and Mercy Missy Napkins.

Because you have a young sounding voice you finally land an interview. Looking around you begin to wonder if this is actually an interview, or maybe you were invited as an example of what could be if these young guys and gals don't play the interview game by the inflexible rules. Your folding chair squeaks from the squirming.

Our great nation has fabricated a Great Society by blending all the melting-pot of newcomers, and has created some wonderful children ... so-far. The Beat Generation of *Zen.*; the Age of Aquarius *or Where are we;* The Boomer's Generation of *Now*; The X-Generation of *Whatever*; and they all boil down to the Skip Generation: *Us*, the cream at the top of the pot.

The 500 skeptically intelligent and superficially compassionate people we've elected to rent homes in Washington D. C., and who qualified for their jobs by passing a political opinion poll in the comics section, are no help. They throw around a lot of words to get votes. We have not been defined and our jobs have not been invented yet; they have not trickled down yet, because we do not need work, they say, we are not expected to work, they believe. We have been skipped.

A pleasant voice finally sings in demonic harmony through the waiting room and calls your name. You rise and a recent-undergraduate young lady beckons you to follow her through the gates of hell, the interview room: As you follow her, pleas echo through your mind, 'Please don't ask me my age. I'll have to lie, and then I'll have to explain how I could be in the Army and Grade School at the same time. Don't ask me my favorite song or singer because that certainly will date me as a Civil War Veteran'. In the cubicle, you become the perfect interviewee.

Your tie is straight, you've swallowed your gum, cell phone is turned off, and you've laid out the correct resume ... out of four you had to concoct depending upon your experience as related to the prospective job. You answer all her questions while looking directly into her eyes and avoid the trap, the distracting movie posters hung on the walls.

Then, "Thank you for coming in. We'll call you when we have an opening you qualify for."

"...But?"

If You <u>Must</u> Work to Have Fun

Major Reasons for Working in Retirement:

Need the money desperately	61%
Desire to stay mentally alert & alive	54%
Need the health benefits if available	52%
Desire to stay physically active	49%
Desire to be 'maybe' useful	47%
Desire to do something fun or enjoyable	37%
Desire to help people, including me	29%
Desire to listen to other people's jokes	24%
Desire to learn new-fangled things	17%
Desire to chase a dream/nightmare	14%

Roughly based on AARP Study Attitudes of Individuals 50 and older toward Phased Retirement online poll of 2.167 workers over 50 March 2005

Bad-Hair Days

(Victims of Murphy's Law)

Most of us deserve the high-quality kind of luck that brings a random chance for prosperity and good fortune. It just takes one lucky day in a lifetime to be somebody else. Some people have it, but most of us don't. We have bad-hair days, we all do, and in all justice we should do something about it, because some of us have those days most of the year. You know who you are, and not those of you with frightening combovers, split ends whipping you on the back like a cat o'nine tails, or frizzy curls undomesticated and maddening.

It is the majority of us who pat the decades on the shoulder as they pass us by and believe good fortune has been left outside in someone else's sunshine ... while it rains all over us inside. "It's just one of those days", has become a daily mantra.

We are the victims of *Murphy's Law*. It is a fact and not just an old saying, "If anything can go wrong, it will." There should be some kind of cosmic balance to this phenomenon. There are so many of us on this side of the luck scale that we have what seem like normal-hair days, and those on the sunshine side are freaks of nature. While THEY win the lottery or are four steps ahead when the truck barreling down the street hits the mud puddle near the curb, we lose and are splashed. That is the odds-in-your-favor existence always left to glow under someone else's sun.

But, again, we should do something about it, but a march on Washington DC won't do the trick; besides, most of us don't have the extra change for airfare anyhow. And don't duplicate the actions of one woman. She received a bad haircut at her local salon: This is a bad-hair day in the real sense of the word. The next day she came back with a pistol, demanded her $100 back, shot up the beauticians car, and went down the street to another salon to have her hair repaired. The best guess, she probably will be spending a lot of bad-hair days in the gray-bar hotel.

There is quite a variety of old sayings that try to smooth ruffled feathers (hair). "We have to play the hand we're dealt." "It all evens out in the end." And the favorite, "What goes around comes around." What the heck does that mean? Does it mean on days when you feel like a dog chasing its own tail, you're OK? Does it mean that someday you will catch it? Then what? Will you find the pot of gold at the end of the rainbow or just another good saying? These are all nice feel-good sayings that function as pacifiers, but only work about as long as it takes to shoot up a beautician's car.

What can we do? We could start by ignoring that disgruntled Irishman, Murphy, and follow the advice of another distinguished philosopher, Simon. Simon says, "If anything can wrong, and does, pay no attention to it and chalk it up to experience."

It is well known that there are some of us who play the same Lottery numbers every week, and the one week we forget to buy a ticket, they draw our numbers. Now that's a bona fide bad-hair day and hard to ignore after you've jumped up and down on the coffee table and created a piece of pulp art. But, all in all, it is a real character building experience – isn't it?

Luck is all relative anyhow. If you win $100 at the local casino, you say "WOW!" If someone in the stratosphere of Mr. Gates or Trump wins the same prize, their reaction would probably be "That's nice, another drop in the bucket." These are both acts of good luck, so luck is just in the eye of the beholder.

Some of us see others gliding along through life like a silk butterfly in a slight breeze without a care in the world. Most of us feel like a caterpillar crawling along in the fast lane of a freeway dodging tires. If we can only make it to the off ramp we may turn into a butterfly. "Hope springs eternal".

All in all if bad-hair days build character, and that's what we like to tell ourselves, then most of us have positive qualities to spare, and we're all candidates for sainthood.

We've endured the worst of days and are now trying to enjoy the best of days. There is nothing we can do to change it now. We can look back at the scrapes and scuffs, black eye, and a broken arm; a car accident or two; sickness here and there; the lost loves; the lost keys; the lost lotteries; the fact that Ed McMahon never delivered your million-dollar check; and the reality that you were born and grew up less than tall, and know you must take it all "with a grain of salt". You know you'll move on.

You'll comb your hair every day, shampoo when you feel like it, get a haircut once a month, pretend your hair is good, and croon a little show tune, "Luck be a Lady tonight."

Senior Quote:

"The most fun thing I have done since my retirement in 1999 is what I'm doing now: participating in a writing workshop, Life Writing, at Story Studio Chicago, and actually doing some writing"...

Marlys: Chicago, IL.

Cool

(Or: Some things get better with age)

You most certainly remember saying it as a youngster, I'm sure … and your parents probably did as well. It's the best way to say something is neat-o, awesome, or swell, or just plain nice or OK. The phrase *cool* is very relaxed, never goes out of style, and no one ever laughs at you for using it; very convenient for people who don't give a rat about what's "in". Sometimes you use it when you don't have a clue about a subject, yet want to act as if you know-it-all, or just sound "hip". Admit it.

"*Cool*" has been with us as an acceptable, universal slang for years. Some things never change. The usage of *cool* as a general positive epithet or interjection has been part of the English slang since before World War II, and has even been lent to other languages, such as French and German. Originally it was a development from a Black English usage meaning "excellent, superlative," first recorded in written English in the early '30s. Jazz musicians who used the term made it popular during the '40s.

Most slang words haven't had the staying power or universal appeal of *cool*, and that's *cool*; some things just endure and get better with age; like cheese, wine, scotch, some beers, and most people.

Aging with poise is a matter of self value and pleasure. "I'm proud of my age. I'm not going to hide behind a cosmetic persona. I'm aging gracefully, I'm *cool*," should be a mantra chanted each morning while eating your oatmeal laced with lifesaving cinnamon. Or then there is the bumper sticker (there always is about every subject), 'If things get better with age, then I'm nearly fantastic'. Age is an ongoing process; time marches on, its unavoidable, and we get older. It's perpetual motion at a personal level.

However, there are rules if you want to become a fine wine 'someone', and not 'crabapple' vinegar. We age better when we are in high spirits and free of negative shadows. Researchers speculate that positive emotions may directly affect health via chemical and neural responses involved in maintaining a perfect balance between wine and vinegar. Your brain knows the difference. In other words, quit saying, “I can’t do it”, instead say, it would be something *cool* to try.

Hints: creativity knows no age limits. In fact, there comes a certain freedom with age. You can create whatever you want. You aren’t at the mercy of the marketplace. You serve your own spirit by letting it have its say. Your years, your lines, your scars are part of who you are. They should be a matter of comfort and pride and even your joy and a foundation for creativity.

And just as age is an ongoing process, so is your sex life. Even if you've been married to the same wacko for decades, sex can be a continuous erotic adventure. And sexual fulfillment helps bring balance into other aspects of our lives, too. And it doesn’t hurt to get that ticker pumping a little faster. *Cool.*

“Age is an issue of mind over matter. If you don't mind, it doesn't matter,” said that former printer's apprentice, Mississippi riverboat pilot, and newspaperman, Mark Twain.

Cool will probably outlive us all, but we may as well hitch a ride on its coat tail while we can. Being *coo*l can make you hot! And better!

? Who are Amos and Andy?

You useta be ...

(Or: The fear of flying into the sixties)

... slimmer, taller, faster, the center of attention, smoother ... less wrinkled, that is ... lighter, tanner, smarter, richer, sexier, at least great deal more romantic, a day dreamer, cooler and less ticked-off all the time, smart as a whip, out on the town more, a loner, on top, well-read, happier, healthier, handier, a better bowler/golfer/hiker or at least more athletic, and even a little more artistic, aesthetic and poetic ... a butcher, a baker, a candlestick maker ... etc.

Most likely the list goes on, and it's a sure thing you've decreed at least one of these minor depreciations of your perfection at one time or another. It's also a solid wager you told some junior humans that you walked to school 2 or 3 miles every day in the snow, rain, and blistering sun. Oh how the truth can be stretched like taffy and shaped like Silly Putty, and that's OK, as long as it has a touch of reality.

"Will you still need me, will you still feed me, when I'm sixty-four", five, six, and so on up the Beatle's scale. That's a good question, now that Boomer era is here or around the corner.

But, moving on, carrying personal memories, tall tales, or baggage from the past into the future, gives you a nice feeling of accomplishment, you doubtless say, it's a pleasant, glowing sensation, but it's just slowing the process of growth into this new era. It's a whole new deal, a new life, an unlimited opportunity. The past is like a chiming ice cream truck pushing you into the future, but if you stop to dwell on it, admire it, it will run over you and leave you like a puppet with no strings, a ragged, limp future, and no Popsicle. It's a good thing, something to be proud of, but you can't drag history with you, like, that is, HOW you are defined as a person, because it will tire you out and you'll miss the present ... and the future.

"Don't watch the clock. Do what it does. Keep going," said Sam Levenson, humorist and writer. 'Keep it going' is good advice. And mentioning 'time' you probably will have a lot more of it to deal with, and fill, with new adventures and wild stories you can use at your next opportunity to tell a whopper to a junior human.

"Do not go gentle into that good night", or the future as far as that goes; time management, planning, and things to do with that extra time are things to seriously consider. So what if your not what you useta be, but you are-what-you-are. So what if you are a little heavier and slower, give up the flag-football Sundays. If you aren't well-read the cheapest thing in town is probably a library card.

Two old men in a retirement village were sitting in the reading room and one said to the other, "How do you really feel? I mean, you're 75 years old, how do you honestly feel?" "Honestly, I feel like a new born baby. I've got no hair, no teeth, and I just peed myself." Now that's taking too much of the past with you ... a little too far. The more things change the more they stay the same, is the title of some albums and an insane political saying. Don't believe it.

The fear of flying into the sixties and beyond is a natural anxiety; after all, it's a whole new world of different, faster, more universal, and exciting things to discover, make use of, explore, and bring into your new lifestyle. 'Life is like riding a bike; you don't fall off unless you stop pedaling,' said a Mr. Pepper. Soon you may be able to say, I useta be afraid, but now I'm having a better life riding a bike.

FREE ... a Fixed Price or Down Payment?

(Or: An assault on your nest egg)

As a penny-wise and future frugal spender of a life-time stash called a 'nest egg', you must save a buck or two, of course. Offers for FREE goods and services are daily being stuffed into mail boxes and e-mails, crushingly pushed through TV screens, falling like snowflakes from magazines, and attached to every web page visited while browsing the cyber world. And, if you accept these offers as honest, you may never part with another penny, for anything ... for life. Be on guard.

What is FREE? You're not imprisoned or shackled, and not under the control of another's will, except by a Better Half, of course, who may impose house arrest, so *set me free* mostly doesn't apply here; you hope. That only leaves the option that someone is going be a generous and overwhelmingly kind spirit and give you something at no cost, no money, gratis, that is, complimentary, you hope.

For example, you've seen it, an ordinary 4x6 pre-addressed postcard trickles from a magazine and floats to the floor like a graceful and disarming dove. After it alights from its flight, the blazing red letters rise from the card like a ruthless hawk and shout "FREE". After inspecting the details of this blazon invitation, it appears 10 issues of the magazine are TRULY FREE for the mere act of ordering a subscription for 30 issues at a low cost of dollars-plus-change. At this low per-issue rate, the card advices, you are getting 10 issues for FREE. More like a down payment. Some deal, huh?

On TV the genteel salesperson warbles a spiel,

"A FREE bottle of magic liquid cleaner ... just buy one bottle and we will send you a second one FREE ... and we will also send you two FREE bottles of shoe dye, the color of your choice, a FREE sponge on a stick, two all-purpose rags, and an entry form that entitles you to enter a contest that offers a FREE trip to Orlando as first prize. And if you order now ..."

It goes on,

..."for each future order you will receive 2 bottles for the price of 1 ... for life"

WOW, all this for just purchasing one 20 oz. bottle of supernatural cleaner for a dirt-low-price plus *Shipping & Handling. (Whatz that?).*

Now another scam (offer) that is closely related to the magazine deal is the book-club offer whispering from a gorgeous brochure personally addressed and slipped into the mailbox: First book, FREE; second book, FREE, third book, by golly, FREE (WOW!); fourth book at the Regular Price plus *Shipping & Handling (OOPS!).* All this for just signing up for a year's supply of other and more books you may or may not order or fancy. FREE in this case is definitely a down payment on future reading activities and an iron clad guarantee of less space in the bookshelf.

Now in most cases *Shipping* charges we can see and understand. The product must get from there to you, somehow, but *Handling* charges are a mystery. Does this imply they wear clean or latex gloves during the packing process? Does this charge guarantee the product *will not be* dented, torn, wrinkled or maimed, and the order *will be* complete, correct and properly addressed? Doubt it! This *handling* charge is probably how they *handle* the lost profit on the FREE part of the offer.

Some things are really and truly FREE ... excluding the obvious; AIR, most of the time. E-mail offers of FREE newsletters are a windfall for penny pinchers. Just sign up for the monthly/weekly/daily e-mail delivery to your inbox of a *newsletter* explaining the values of beatnik poetry or the filling in of the mud flats of Arizona, or something along this order of wisdom. The cool thing is the newsletter will also offer

FREE bargains for everything. That's all. But to sign up you must fill out several web pages of personal information: Hmmmm!

Some other things are FREE: Catalogs, for obvious reasons; CDs with multi-purpose programs to install on your computer are FREE (but SAFE?); Kittens are FREE; Coins are FREE if you want to stand on a street corner with a cup; FREE tips; FREE hand up; and FREE peanuts or popcorn at the bar. FREE INTEREST? (Read the fine print.)

But here is something that is really FREE ... advice; the most important and generally FREE item is your will or self control. You can or cannot, will or will not, must or must not, fall for FREE offers from even the most attractive offerer person who wants to dip into the Nest Egg. Be FREE to say ... NO THANKS.

? Who was Captain Kangaroo before he was Captain Kangaroo?

The Enemies You Buy

(If you can't beat'em, join'em)

You, as a red-blooded and very experienced human being, have always had the self-belief that you were smarter than a toaster. You know the younger generation with all their gizmos and thingamabobs could fry you in a one-on-one contest of technology trivia. But you always thought your discount-store inventory of appliances was a safe haven. You know it's a hard choice between saving money, and saving sanity. But things happen.

Your first morning off and finally in retirement you were rudely attacked from the blind side by a blood-curdling scream that interrupted your canoe ride through a softly tinted forest on a serene stream. Your nighttime dream world had been shattered like a cheap mirror.

Your first reaction was self-defense. You grabbed the pillows and crushed them to the sides of your head, for self-protection, to muffle the eventual mashing of your brain by those ultra-violent sound waves. It only took a few seconds to clear the fog and readjust your wits; so you could analyze how you'd been thrown from your serene stream into the front row of an acid rock concert in hell.

Your second reaction, an automatic motor function, was to open your eyes, blink, then adjust to the daylight and investigate to see if the room was spinning around you or you around it. Your third reaction was descriptive, 'Dagnabit!' If you haven't figured it out, your first enemy of the day was a whirly little electronic black-blazer-butler Made-In-China hammer located somewhere inside your newly purchased inexpensive snooze-alarm-radio clock. Your fourth reaction was to moan, '*why is it screeching, and how do I turn it off.*' You are sure you hadn't turned the alarm on in the first place the night before. You can sleep in these days. That's what you've worked for. You must have placed one of the ten or dozen knobs and switches in the wrong position. You don't punch a clock anymore, but this time you did.

To fix this little box of horrors before the next morning, you set each switch in the desired position, just like the multi-language instructional pamphlet suggests, secured them into position with a lump of Scotch Tape, and said a little prayer to Thomas Edison, who you're sure, is the God of electronics.

The coffee pot was a mostly harmless, but a sometimes sneaky, enemy. You ran water into the coffee pot, placed a new clean white filter into the little basket with the magical hole at the bottom, measured in the proper ratio of coffee grounds per cup of water, poured in the exact amount of water, anticipating a little extra boost to help your forget the morning's dashed dreams, closed it all up, and pushed the brew button.

You could hear the babbling and singing of the coffee maker. About once a week, or so, it's an accepted disaster, one of the sides of the nice new white paper filter will collapse and allow pure, unsaturated, gritty bits of ground coffee to pass through the magic hole and into the pot. And So! The first cup you pour in that morning looks like a mud puddle in a freshly turned garden plot with dirt floating around the edges like baby bugs.

Again, you have three choices of defense to act out here: First, you could yell Dagnabit! which you already know solves nothing; Second, you know lumps of Scotch Tape won't work in this situation, so you can either repeat the steps above for a new pot; or Third, you can give ground (no pun intended) to the enemy and attempt to dab up the grit from the suspicious liquid with the corner of a paper towel. Next time, you muttered, you'll remember to inspect the filter like your

Army Captain used to scrutinize your footlocker. Another option is pay the extra bucks for quality filters.

In the meantime, the new toaster, the one with the unpretentious knob that assigns *Light* to the left, and *Dark* to the right, and neither means anything anyhow, smoked like a three-alarm fire in the corner of the kitchen cabinet, contentedly and warmly creating black tiles of bread. Enough said! You won't get into the color of the butter as you took up the challenge and tried to spread it with non-crumbling agility across the flat sides of the tiles. This enemy is easy to defeat, but may take a whole loaf of bread. Starting from the left you toasted slices of bread until the exact color mix of $700-dollar-an-ounce gold and charcoal was attained. Then, with a dab of enamel paint (nail polish will do) you marked the spot for perfect toast ... just in case someone turns the knob. Toast quality is personal choice and not an exact science.

The bowl of oatmeal gruel in the microwave had just bubbled and exploded. This enemy is a subtle sniper. The muted hum of the electromagnetic waves rattled your breakfast into an edible temperature zone and lulled you into a sense of false security. The muted crack of an explosion rocked the morning air like a sniper's gunshot. You'd overlooked the warning sign: *Cover All Food*. The inside of the zap contraption looked like your enemy had layered stucco on the walls with a paint gun filled with gray matter. You'd forgotten to put a cover over the bowl. Never do that. Just a paper plate over the top would be easy, and is disposable.

Your enemies started to resemble you.

Warning here, Juicers are armed land mines if the lid is taken off too soon, unless you want to wear a shirt with an orange-spatter pattern.

These lessons were disturbing for someone like you who was trying to be a non-morning person and sleep in, relax, read, and all that. Your enemies were lurking in every doodad convenience gadget you bought at the discount store. It's part of the deal and clearly printed within the barcode you can't read, also on the label you can't remove from your appliance without a blowtorch or strong acid. You've found, just because these appliances were cheap and have been designed with all the friendly colors and curves, it doesn't make them friendly, let alone trustworthy.

Well then, if you can't beat them, you figured you should join them. You've learned to fix and work around all these appliance attacks, and passed the information along to friends. It has built for you the reputation as the Appliance Guy: There are many enemy appliances lurking out there, this is just a sampling. It could be that new hobby you were looking for. You won't make much money, but free coffee and lunch in exchange for that small appliance repair or hints will be an entertaining hobby, and if you join the enemy and get good at it, you can make lots of friends.

? Who the Little Beaver?

Vital Statistics

(Crunching Numbers into the Future)

There are hundreds of polls, if not a gazillion, supported by massive heaps of data, stats and whispers of opinions circulating this rock called earth, and thumbing through piles of publications reveals their existence. Some of these stats are amusingly funny facts, and some are deliriously serious.

The hard-working number crunchers inform the giving-up-work gang about who you are, should be, want to be, ought to be, why, and why not. They suggest plans of how much cash you should produce, actually get, squander, what to fritter it away on, what you actually waste it on and with whom, and how much to expend and when. In addition, they calculate where you should live, do live, with whom, and for how long: And on and on.

Numbers nerds produce statistics like rabbits on the blue pill produce rabbits, and spin the digits into pyramid piles, apple pie charts, and bar and grill graphs.

Generally, though, there is little you can do about most of the numbers they conjure up, so fretting is not an option. But thinking about some of them can direct you to where you reside in the pecking order of the big human picture. Like this, we've heard that 77 million Boomers started retiring in 2006: Nothing we can do about that, but this may cause strains on Social Security, Medicare and mega-long lines at public restrooms, and we hope-after-hope there are no soup lines.

Other studies show Americans shrink between one and two inches between the ages of 30 to 70. Can't do anything about the inch or two lost except buy smaller clothes and hope you don't shrink so much you no longer qualify to take the rides at the amusement park. Growing feet of the elderly is another, nothing you can do about the expanding human pedestal pads except purchase longer and wider shoes.

Specifically, though, you ought to be responsive to some of the personal and significant vital statistics you can control, such as, weight, blood pressure, glucose level, bowling average, golf handicap, balancing the checkbook, and how long it takes to cook a three-minute egg. And then, how many calories you shed on that morning walk/jog, and how many you re-figure into your bottom line with the Danish pastry at the coffee shop after the exercise. These everyday concerns must be mastered and monitored to continue clowning around with the retirement set forever and a day, as they say.

Then there are critical concerns like: 85% of the entomologists (zoologist who study insects) at the USDA Forest Service are expected to retire soon. This could be very significant to those of you who retire solely with the purpose of populating your ant farms from National Parks. Who knows where those ants have been if they haven't been closely watched.

A number of other datum thoughts for the day – There is more money spent on breast implants and Viagra than on Alzheimer's research. This means that by 2030, there will be a large elderly population with perky boobs and huge erections and absolutely no recollection of what to do with them, and that is scary. 27% of women say they get a good night's sleep, 38% of men say they do. Man, your snoring is keeping the Lady awake. 1.3% of Americans 65 and older experience major depressive episodes, compared with 10% of 18- to 49-year olds. Some things do get better with age and experience.

History and statistics prove 100% of your money will outlive you, although not necessarily in your possession. So spending it now is a statically beneficial option. Then again, until your number is up, don't worry. "There are lies, damned lies and statistics", quoth the wise old-timer, Mark Twain.

Below is a mishmash of statistics collected over time from various sources and publications, and relate to whether or not we will have fun in retirement. As mentioned before, some are funny facts, and some are deliriously serious.

- 25% of American adults 50 and older believe they have a 'sleep problem,' (Gallup Survey -- Taken from AARP Bulletin December 2005)
- 28% of Americans 65 and older had annual incomes of less than $10,000 in 2004.
- By the year 2030, the U.S. Census Bureau projects, the U.S. population will grow to 363 million, up from 281 million 2000.
- Older Americans are less interested in aging than younger ones. However, in a USA Today/ABC News survey they also found that on an average Americans want to live to be 87. That definitely defies the laws of averaging which says that is 9 years older than the current life expectancy of 78. (Taken from AARP Bulletin December 2005)
- Because of aging, populations are putting a burden on public finances, and I suppose public restrooms, too, it has been suggested that people are encouraged to stay at work longer, that is retire later, to ease the overburdened work force. In addition, I suppose to pay more taxes.
- The average woman born between 1946 and 1964 will probably have to work until age 74 as a theater cashier or a hand shaker in a chain store.
- 58% of women in the baby-boomer generation have less than $10,000 saved in a pension or 401(k) plan, with an additional few dollars of pennies in a jelly jar near the cookies jar jammed with nickels.
- 87% of the impoverished elderly are women.

- In 2004 Americans spent $20 billion on various anti-aging products.
- 69% of adults over 50 use the internet at least occasionally to look for health information. (AARP Bulletin)
- According to the latest data from the NPD Group, 28% of men and 24% of women over 65 eat nuts at least one a week, compared with just 13% of adults under 65. (Does this mean we turn to squirrels as we grow older?)
- For a 30 minute period 127 calories are burned walking, and 173 are burned swing dancing.
- 10% of workers 55 to 64 are self-employed.
- 39.5% of American Women 65 and older are kept out of poverty by Social Security.

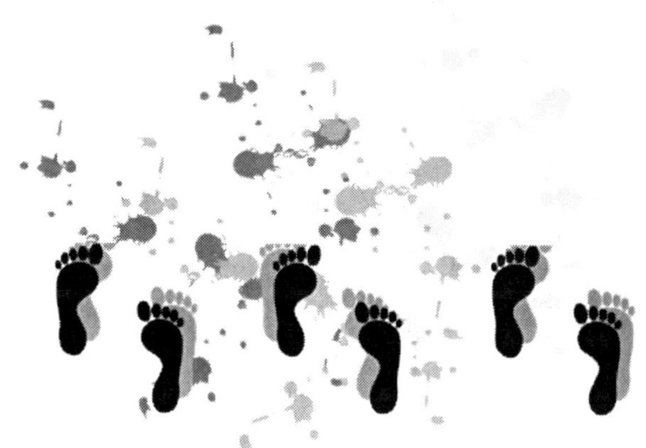

Sixth: Fun Day Trips

Following are some suggestions for filling that spare time in those long and sometimes thumb-twiddling days off by; getting a little exercise, seeing the sights, breathing outside air, connecting with nature and other people, and maybe learning something new-fangled along the way. Maybe take your camera one day and bring back the memories: *Walking Excursions*; *Bar Hopping* (short hops, of course), *Art Walks*; *Touring Yard Sales*; and *Day Hikes* are some of the safest trips. Then there are shorter trips, and the shortest is a trip to your computer to *Cruise the Senior Internet*.

Walking excursions:

A wild and original couple in Seattle had conjured up the project of walking around Lake Washington, mile by mile, day by day. They would drive to the lake, walk a mile up the shoreline, and then back to their car. The next day they would park where they left off the day before and walk another mile, and back to their car.

Just to get an idea of how big the project is, driving the freeway from the North end of the lake, Kenmore, to the south end, Renton, is about 24 miles. Double that for going down the other side and include all the inlets and bays that jag along the shoreline and you get the picture. It is a long walk. They devised this project to pass the time, get fresh air, and exercise every day. You can make up you own, I am sure.

There are so many places to take in the city nature hikes, such as the White River in Indianapolis near the Broad Ripples District, or even the Canal Walk in its Downtown District. The 25 mile Greenbelt along the Boise River in Boise Idaho is alive with wild life, and people walking and biking to town for work. You can even ride your bike along these trails if you want to.

Along the river you can see ducks with ducklings, frogs hopping across the trail, dragon flies dodging and darting, birds skirting the trees and chirping their morning songs, and you know what, even other people who say Good Morning or Hi! The flow of the river creates a soothing mantra that will relax any beast that lives inside you, and the sun flashing between the tree branches and trunks is just hypnotic enough to take off the edge.

Then there is the shorter 2-mile walk in Portland, Oregon, next to the Willamette River. They advise that it is about a 40 minute walk, or 70 minutes with pubs. This walk has Pubs and Dining as well as a waterfront and possibly can be combined with the next topic, Bar Hopping.

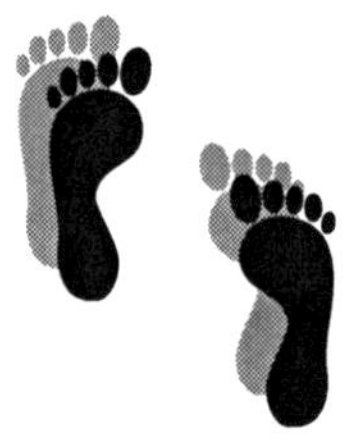

Bar hopping:

This daily trip can come together with *Walking* or *Biking*, but not *Window Shopping*; you must go into the business, and not driving: you must be able to get home without a DUI incident. Pick a long city street and start at the first bar or tavern at one end. Each day you must enter, have one (maybe two at the most) beer(s), talk to the bartender, and maybe the customer next to you, introduce yourself, and meet someone new.

The following day stop at the next bar down the street. On this trip, you can go up one side of the street to the end, then come back, or zigzag back and forth. Doing this trip as a couple makes it much more interesting because you can compare notes each day. The downside here is you have to avoid talking to each other in the bar and concentrate on the mission of talking to new people. After the end of the trip, you can either pick a different street, or apply for your PHD in psychological therapy and hang out a shingle, *'Bar Talk Specialist'*. Better yet, keep a log, and write a book.

Some things don't change and can take all the fun out of this activity. The down side to this fun task is the 100 calories in a lite bottle of beer, and up to 175 calories in a regular. Here is where you will probably have to combine *Walking* or *Biking*, or some other activity, and *Bar Hopping*. If you weigh 160 pounds and walk a mile at 4 mph, you can burn 94 calories. If you are a smaller person weighing 100 pounds, you will have to walk and mile at 7 mph. Below is a demoralizing chart or two to refer to and judge how much **fun** you really want to have in each bar, and what the **penalty** is going to be.

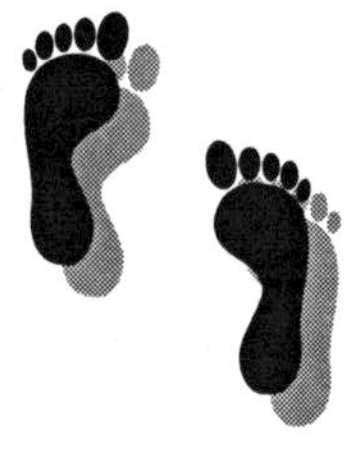

Art walks

Las Vegas has a First Friday; The City of Laguna Beach, California has a 1st Thursday; Portland, Maine also has a First Friday; Boise, Idaho has a First Thursday, and Downtown Los Angeles has a Second Thursday. And again, Scottsdale, Arizona has one every Thursday; Second Friday in Carrboro and Chapel Hill, North Carolina; a Second Saturday in Sacramento, California; a Third Thursday in Edmonds, Washington; Atlanta, Georgia has a First Thursday, and again, First Friday in Phoenix, Arizona.

It appears every city has an organized or disorganized Arts Walk, and I am positive there is one lying in wait for you to examine. If you have the time and the money, I am sure you could round out a good month by *Arts Walk Hopping* from city to city and town to town throughout North America. Most of us have the time, but not the money for airfare or the fortitude to ride all those busses.

If you live in a large city, you can organize your own mini Arts Walk for yourself or with a few friends. Select an area of the city and go Arts Walking there for the day and for frills and fun throw in a lunch at a new café.

Not every day, but several times a week, and by the end of the month, most galleries have changed their shows and you can repeat the above. This is just as good a way to exercise as walking around a lake or hopping from bar to bar, and much more sobering.

Everybody probably has an art walk in or near them. Probably a simple Google search like: YOURCITY Art Walk will probably get you close to a web page with all the information you need.

More information for each of the Arts Walks mentioned above is at their web site:

- Laguna Beach – http://www.firstthursdaysartwalk.com/

- Portland, Maine – http://www.firstfridayartwalk.com/
- Downtown Los Angeles – http://www.downtownartwalk.com/
- Scottsdale, Arizona – http://www.scottsdalegalleries.com/
- Carrboro and Chapel Hill, North Carolina – http://www.scottsdalegalleries.com/
- Sacramento, California – http://www.sacramento-second-saturday.org/
- Edmonds, Washington – http://www.edmondswa.com/Events/ArtWalk/index.html
- Atlanta, Georgia – http://www.atlantadowntown.com/HavingFun_FirstThursdays.asp
- Phoenix, Arizona – http://www.artlinkphoenix.com/templates/index.php
- Boise, Idaho – http://www.downtownboise.org/m_events/dba_first_thursday.cfm
- Las Vegas, Nevada – http://www.firstfriday-lasvegas.org/

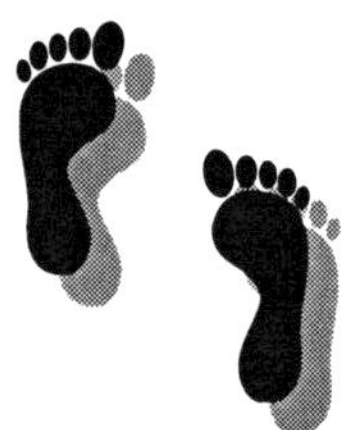

Touring Yard Sales

In a slice of life essay above you were instructed how to, or how not to, generate a yard sale. Now explore the other side of the table and shop at the yard sales. Four rules: If you want to buy something, bring money; if you don't want to be suckered in by some dusty gotta-have-it knickknack, don't bring money, or credit cards; or if you are just looking, bring your eyes and your glasses; remember this is just somebody else's junk.

Day Hikes

OK, if it's late spring or summer or early autumn the snow is off the mountains and there are no more excuses or pleading to the Gods of TV to let you be. In fact, the sun is about to blister the gooseberry leaves off the alumroot mountain flowers and drive the animals down into the food-inviting parks. So, take their place in the high hills for a day, eat their food ... although I don't know how tasty tree bark or dandelion seed heads would be.

'Mountains,' you say? Well, day hikes can also be taken rimming some valleys, along rivers or around lakes ... level land. Mountain trail is sometimes just the name for a dusty dirt trail that is not a sidewalk.

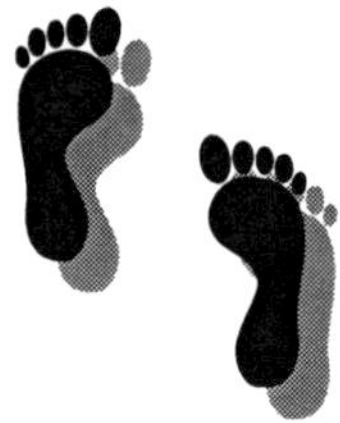

Calories burned per mile by walking

Weight in Pounds								
	Pounds	100	120	140	160	180	200	220
Speed	2.0 mph	65	80	93	105	120	133	145
	2.5 mph	62	74	88	100	112	124	138
	3.0 mph	60	72	83	95	108	120	132
	3.5 mph	59	71	83	93	107	119	130
	4.0 mph	59	70	81	94	105	118	129
	4.5 mph	69	82	97	110	122	138	151
	5.0 mph	77	92	108	123	138	154	169
	6.0 mph	86	99	114	130	147	167	190
	7.0 mph	96	111	128	146	165	187	212

Calories per hour burned by bike riding

	140 lbs.	195 lbs.
Bicycling, 10-11.9 mph, light effort	381	531
Bicycling, 12-13.9 mph, moderate effort	508	708
Bicycling, 14-15.9 mph, vigorous effort	636	885
Bicycling, 16-19 mph, very fast, racing	763	1062
Bicycling, >20 mph, racing	1017	1416
Bicycling, Mountain or BMX	540	753
Bicycling, stationary, general	318	443
Bicycling, stationary, very light effort	191	266
Bicycling, stationary, light effort	330	487
Bicycling, stationary, moderate effort	445	620
Bicycling, stationary, vigorous effort	667	930
Bicycling, stationary, very vigorous effort	795	1107

To find out the calories burned in various activities, go to the Health Status online Calories Burned Estimator:

http://www.healthstatus.com/calculate/cbc

Cruising the Senior Internet

No fresh air here, unless you bring your laptop to the backyard or a park, but it's great no-sweat fun if you can't walk, jog, bike, climb, shop, bowl or drink beer for a hobby. You can sit firmly attached to a comfortable seat with coffee or the beverage of your choice, a muffin or chocolate dipped pretzels, and enjoy non-private conversations with people from the four corners of the world.

If you have time on your hands, and some of us do, and possess a pretty good computer with one-speed, a two-button palm-sized mouse (maybe with an optional speed-scroll wheel), and are driving your modem-powered computer throughout the world-wide internet, then you may as well detour and join any one of several very friendly senior chat groups ... or all of them if you are curious about every angle of every imaginable subject matter.

Now cruising can mean sailing the seas on a pleasure trip; seeking a sexual partner on a Saturday night spin around town; or just plain allowing your mind to wander in the fantasies of yourself and others. Have you ever had something to say, and no one to say it to? Then put your mental top down, let the virtual reality blow through your hair, and participate.

They exchange jokes (clean and evocative), recipes, health hints, insults, marriage proposals, local weather, household suggestions for everything from opening that love letter, not to you, but to your mate (without being detected), doubling up on SOS pad usage, and the many household remedies cured by the wonder-cleaner Alka-Seltzer tablets. Political views from international perspectives are freely opined and exchanged and sometimes you will shine your headlights up a different road.

And the good things about this: you don't have to duck a punch after you state your political opinion. And another good thing about this: you don't have to smell his bad breath or BO. Of course, on the other hand, you don't have to gargle, brush your teeth or even dress while chatting on the net. As Peter Steiner put it in one of his cartoons in The New Yorker, "On the Internet, no one knows you're a dog."

"Do you have a sense of humor, a wide range of interests and shoot from the lip? For serious discussion and wonderful silly nonsense join us on HG (Hells Geriatrics), the over fifties forum for those who think." This is the description that comes from a group at: http://groups.yahoo.com/group/HellsGeriatrics/

"Welcome everyone!! Jump in and post and enjoy the group. Look forward to hearing from everyone!" This is the description for the group at: http://groups.yahoo.com/group/strolldownmemorylane/

"*Retired Old Farts* is a group of young-at-heart retired persons who have in common being retired, being on the internet and having a sense of humor. (Plus others who convinced the Founder that they deserved to belong.) Many of us on ROF have delighted in *being silly* and making up our own private world with Our Laird and his castle." This is the introduction copy for the site: http://groups.yahoo.com/group/rof2/

These are just a few of the available sites and they are having fun. Or, if these don't fit your style, start your own and see where it heads. Also be prepared, as you are cruising, for the input of lists and tests, like: The Official Nerd Test, or The Top 20 Reasons Chocolate Is Better than Sex, or celebrating your birthday with a byte candlelight dancing cake. Don't be shy. Cruise the sites with your windows open and get a feel for the atmosphere. Then send a message introducing yourself. You'll be surprise at how many friends you will make ... real fast.

"A man's errors are his portals of discovery," said Francis Bacon. And there you have it, portals of discovery, the foundation for these sites and the resulting claptrap circling the world.

Thanks for the 'very exciting' day trips

Maybe a day trip experience that shouldn't be taken: "I've sure gotten old. I've had two by-pass surgeries, a hip replacement, and new knees ... fought prostate cancer, and diabetes. I'm half blind, can't hear anything quieter than a jet engine, take 40 different medications that make me dizzy, winded, and I'm subject to blackouts. Have bouts with dementia. Have poor circulation; and hardly feel my hands and feet anymore. Can't remember if I'm 85 or 92 and have lost all my friends.

But ... Thank God for small miracles, I still have my Florida driver's license!"

Seven: Important People In Your Life

Following are rare interviews and studies captured on tape, pencil and the unstable memory of writers and other questionable people. It is important in pursuing the nirvana of fun in retirement by inquiring what the longtime residents of the emotion say, believe, and how they got there.

Grouch and Cranky are always good for insightful revelations of the human spirit, and *An Interview with Mother Nature* tells the tales of things we can't control. *Centenarians* are a coming force to reckon with, and *His and Her Towels* expose the great divide among humans of different attitudes.

Grouchy and Cranky

(Can't we all just get along?)

If you haven't caught on by now to the differences between Grouchy Old Men and Cranky Old Ladies, you'd better catch up if your senior years are going to be any fun at all ... and if you're going to survive them. It is not just an item of gossip, or a well-worn joke, but a completely exact adage, *men and women are different.*

Of course you are aware, to be utterly open and honest, it has already been cautiously proven in the Chemistry Laboratory at Any Old U. that the properties of the male and female species are totally different ... and this should come as a surprise, WHY? In the first place we've already been told they come from different planets, Violent Venus and Mild Mars.

The chemical element name for females is *Woman (HER)*, or sometimes called *Cranky*. Their atomic weight is not to be analyzed or talked about by husbands or friends. Crankys have physical elements that are generally round in form, they boil at the drop of a man's hat, may freeze up at any time or anyplace, melt whenever treated nice, but are bitter if not used properly. They are an active and highly unstable element and possess a strong attraction toward rare metals and precious gemstones.

Crankys are violent when left alone, and turn tainted green when placed next to a better HER specimen, or after consuming huge portions of exotic food; like pizza, pork rinds, and real beer. They prone to accessorize and are an excellent means for thinning out someone's wealth and are probably the most powerful income reducing agent known to man. They become violent when left alone, and should arrive with a caution label that warns they are a highly explosive element.

The element name for the polar opposite, males, is *Man (HIM)*, or sometimes called *Grouchy*. Atomic weight = 180+. They are solid at room temperature but bulge out of shape easily over time, are fairly dense but sometimes flaky. Examination has found it is difficult to find a pure sample of a Grouchy. Because of age and rust, the older samples are unable to conduct energy as well as the younger samples. They all have an amorous attraction and insatiable desire to bond with HER any chance they can get. They also tend to form strong social and sports bonds with other Grouchys and become explosive when mixed with Kid (IT) for prolonged periods of time. They can be neutralized by being saturated with alcohol, and are a good source for methane gas. They also come with a caution label that warns, if left without contact or guidance from HER they rapidly begin to decompose and start to smell.

Science has also found that the combining and separating of these two elements has created all the byproduct elements for country songs and Middle Ages sonnets, and have charged ions that transmit TV programs such as the Dating Game and Divorce Court.

It also has been proven after years of mixing and matching, poking and pawing, and scientific observation that a Grouchy is just a happier person. What else can you expect from such simple creatures? His last name stayed the same when he was married, besides, Cranky's wedding dress cost 5-grand, but Grouchy's tux was a hundred-buck rental. The wedding plans just happened.

The garage is all Grouchy's, as well as all the junk in it, and the rest of the house belongs to Cranky to care for and clean. Car mechanics tell Grouchys the straight dope, and they don't have to stop and think of which way to turn a nut on a bolt. They know stuff about taxes and tanks and they've played with toys all their life. They can never be pregnant. They can wear a white T-shirt to a water park. They can wear NO shirt to a water park.

On the other hand, Cranky doesn't have to design the occasional perfect belch. New shoes may cut, blister, or maim them for life, but they bear the pain to preserve their existence in an upper social stratosphere. Phone conversations last much longer than 30 seconds. They open most of their jars by passing them on to Grouchy. Underwear costs more than $8.95 for a three-pack and feels better the more it costs. Everything on their face stays its original color as long as the bottles or tubes aren't empty. The same hairstyle has lasted for years, maybe decades, but has only changed color and length and wave.

The scientific conclusion will make you happy, depending upon which restroom door you pass through:

Grouchy is happier, but Cranky lives longer. Go Figure.

Senior Quote:

"The most fun thing I have done since retirement? WIFE SWAPPING ... the most surprisingly fun thing I have found out about retirement ... WIFE SWAPPING ... and new hobbies or activities after retirement ... WIFE SWAPPING" ...

John: Stepford, CA.

An Interview with Mother Nature

We're here in the lobby of a mid-west hotel lately leveled by an uninvited guest, Tornado. The pillars that once propped the upper floors are still standing ... sort of, but the remainder of the hotel is tossed along the interstate blended with the remains of a trailer park salad. I'm in a dusty overstuffed chair and Mother Nature is blowing above me like a Chinook Chopper.

Question: Thank you, Mother Nature, for making time in your busy schedule to talk to me. Most people consider you, the oldest woman in the world, the real *Person of the Year* and they want to hear from you. Tell me Mother Nature, before we start, do you prefer to be called Ms. Nature, Mrs. Nature or just plain Mother?

Mother Nature: Well, actually I like to be called Big Mother, Big Momma, or Big Mahthah. Whatever you feel comfortable with.

Question: Well, OK, Big Mother, We'll call you BM for the interview. If that's (Mrs.) Mother Nature, where is Mister Nature these days. He isn't mentioned much in the almanacs, on CNN, or even the weather reports?

Big Mother: There is none. Never has been, never will be. It's Miss Nature if you want to get technical about the social fine points. And I don't go for that Ms. hokey-pokey jazz infused into the language by lonely females with nothing else to do.

Q: Wow, Big Mother, isn't that pretty rough criticism of your fellow females?

BM: Yeah, right, if you say so. I've never married. I haven't found anyone large enough or powerful enough to match me blow for blow. I'm not called Big Mother for nothing, you know. I did hunt for a mate around the cosmic and infinite universe during the Ice Age. There wasn't much happening here or much for me to do what with all that boring white snow and ice covering everything. It moved around, but much to slow for a spirited being like me. But with a little help from mankind, I'm upping the speed of the melting process. That could keep me and you guys busy for centuries.

Anyway, I didn't find anyone out there to mate with. Oh, I found a couple of lighter-than-air entities I fooled around with, but I could see right through them, Yuk Yuk: And I'm not kidding about that. They didn't have the muscle or temperament to equal my insatiable appetite. You know what I mean, Pee Wee? But they did provide me with a few of those offspring you see trashing the earth.

Q: But according to the evening news and legend, you are the mother of all we see and feel in nature: Hence the name, Mother Nature, right?

BM: Well, Most of it.

Q: Well, I thought Mother Nature was the over-all and cover-all entity responsible for everything earthly and not human.

BM: Wow! That's a lot to tag on me. I'm not God you know. But that's for another time and another interview.

Q: OK, but as the Big Mother, you must take responsibility for your offspring, Hurricane, Earthquake, Tsunami, Tornado, Volcano, and Flood.

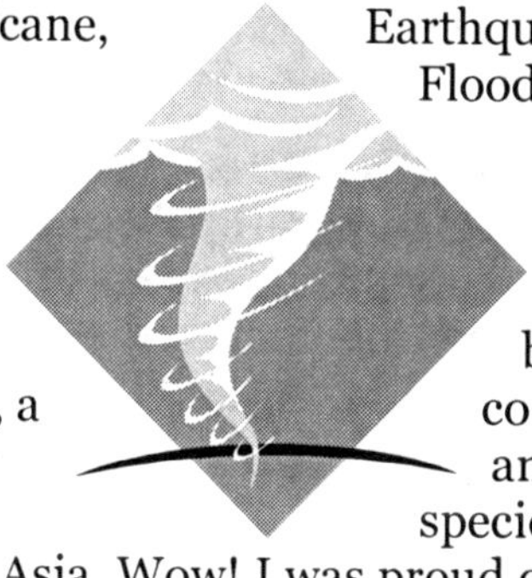

BM: Mean little bastards, aren't they? Take that Tsunami in the Pacific a little while back. What a buster that was. A combination, a co-op undertaking of earthquake, ocean water and a lot of gravity; it really thinned out most species and habitats in those low lying lands off Asia. Wow! I was proud of that child. And my daughter Katrina the Hurricane, she was sensational. Have you heard the saying, 'Don't mess with Mother Nature'? Well, she saw New Orleans fooling around and living under sea level and she decided to issue a warning.

Q: But so many died in those storms ... how can you deal with all the fatalities and destruction you cause? How can you be proud of that?

BM: But it's part of the plan, just my part of the deal. We have to keep populations thinned out so the other elements can survive and not become extinct by over consumption.

Q: What do you mean by 'We'?

BM: Well, you don't think I'm in this alone, do you? Oh, I'm sorry; you're supposed to be asking the questions. Anyway, you don't really hear diddly about the rest of the gang, although they're here every day just like I am. I guess, since I also have a pretty side, you know, like flower, trees, cuddly animals and such, I get a most of the good publicity. But don't ever forget the other Mean Mothers of Famine and Plague. Most people mistake these Mothers as being part of my Nature. They often blame Mother Nature, me, with these functions. But those Mean Mothers have their own job descriptions and responsibilities. But that's another story.

Q: But Big Mother, you are not only known for being the personification of nature as a powerful woman, you are also suppose to be a nurturing woman, that is, someone who gives tender care and protection to living things, young and old. Do you still do that?

BM: Oh Gosh Yes! Of course I do, I try. The only problem is you humans think you own the world and try to control its environment. You can't even control yourselves.

You're an old Dude, Pee Wee, and you live in the richest country on earth, at least temporarily the richest, and you don't even have Health Insurance or someone to look after you. Humans have completely forgotten the Tribal Mores, the family of man has been discarded for bottom-line thinking and the lunatics have taken over the asylum. I have to flex my muscles once in a while to let you know who is really in control.

Q: That's really tough love, Big Mother. But don't you think this is just part of the evolutionary process?

BM: Ahhhh! One of the Big EEEs:

Evolution, Ecology and Economics.

Evolution will move along at its own predestined pace and is not in the hands of humans to control. But the Ecological and Economic factors can be influenced by humans, and right now, they are destroying earth's ecology, MY ECOLOGY, by concentrating on the petty, temporal element of bottom-line profiteering Economics.

Q: Well, you are one tough Momma, and you do seem to have your plate full of activities. Can you give me a hint of what we can expect next?

BM: Now that would take all the fun out of it. Sorry, I have to go now. I see something just over the horizon I have to fix.

? Who says "Wunnerful, Wunnerful, Wunnerful?" And who are his Sisters?

Centenarians

A reporter was interviewing a 104 year-old woman: “And what do you think is the best thing about being 104?” the reporter asked.

She simply replied, “No peer pressure.”

That may not be entirely true these days: In the 1990 census there were a total of 37,306 centenarians (somebody who has live to tell tales and lies past the age of a hundred), living in the United States—and 6,359 of them had celebrated their 105th birthday.

Corroborating with other studies on aging, a larger number of women lived to 100 than men. In fact, four out of five centenarians were women. Eighty-four % of these centenarian women were widowed, compared to 58% who were men.

Taking into consideration population trends thus far, researchers have been able to make estimated projections about future populations of centenarians. According to some, there could be as many as 850,000 centenarians by the year 2,050, creating a wider and more diverse population than ever before. As life expectancy continues to climb, more and more of us will span across centuries.

The lesson learned from these bits of trivia is to plan your fun with retirement very carefully since it likely will last a while. Honorary past members of this elite centenarian group were comedians George Burns and Bob Hope, and you won’t find two better examples of how having fun can make your life longer. For example George said, “First you forget names, then you forget faces. Next you forget to pull your zipper up and finally, you forget to pull it down” Now that’s having fun. And Bob adds, “I'm so old they've cancelled my blood type.”

Two old men in a retirement village were sitting in the reading room at the library and one said to the other, "How do you really feel? I mean, you're almost 100 years old, how do you honestly feel?"

"Honestly, I feel like a newborn baby. I've got no hair, no teeth, and I just peed myself."

?

His and Hers Towels

(Or: Matching "I'm With Stupid" T-Shirts)

Speaking of stolen identity ... as you slink around retirement, arm-in-arm with your soul mate, anticipating nothing but relaxation, excitement and good times, something shadows your golden path ... His and Hers towels, beautifully embroidered with larger-than-life script letters ... may give you a hint.

These are a simple method to finally know which bath towel or bath robe is yours, but ... and this is especially important ... if there are two people living in the same place, with lots of time on their hands, the invasion of personal possessions and areas of comfort in all things will inevitably be the origin of spats, or better, hours or days of silence.

"DON'T WIPE YOUR SHOES WITH MY TOWEL!" or, "KEEP YOUR MAKEUP OFF MY WASHCLOTH!"

Sound familiar? It happens to the best of people. We territorialize our lives. 'After all, if it weren't for marriage, men and women would have to fight with perfect strangers,' said that internationally famous philosopher - Anonymous.

Now, at last, you can stop speculating, if you have, and you may have heard this before, why they build houses with two-car garages, two bedrooms, two baths, a living room the size of Vermont, and both an attic as well as a basement ... a water-grow-mow, water-grow-mow front yard and a back yard with ever-creeping and expanding flower beds: His and Her territories. It is no shocker that male and female brains differ quite a bit in architecture and activity, and it most likely explains why one rearranges the furniture while the other is practices golf around it. The habits and distractions of men and women do differ ... even in retirement ... even after having lived together nearly forever.

You would think after all the years being together couples could learn to live together, and share (you know, using something along with others, in case you've forgotten). Mars and Venus are planets; Mars and Venus are excuses for the differences between a man and woman; Mars and Venus -- Mars is the fourth planet from the Sun and is commonly referred to as the Red Planet: Venus is the second planet from the Sun and the sixth largest planet. Neither place has been occupied by a human of any species as far as we know. Never ... and never is a very long time. End of discussion.

After all, the root of marriage problems as it relates to international affairs was brought to the forefront by a former President with the initials, JFK. "We cannot negotiate with those who say, 'What's mine is mine, and what's yours is negotiable.'" Compromise or 'give-and-take' is often used as a solution to all (most) territorial problems. George Burn and Gracie compromised in their own way. "A lot of husbands appreciate their wife's cooking. I appreciate my wife not cooking." ... It was sort of a compromise or a win-win agreement.

Individualism is an American way of life and is engrained into our lives since birth. It's a hard habit to break. But there are solutions: two-signature checks; bicycles built for two; two-way streets going in opposite directions but down the same road; Tea for Two – or is that coffee for one and tea for the other? Going to a restaurant for dinner on the same night (together); motorcycles with side cars (if you dare), and matching 'I'm With Stupid' T-shirts, all exist to close the gap: Can't we all just get along?

Traveling Seniors

♫ "On the Road Again ..." ♫

Traveling works ... and is in fact much more fun ... once you get out of the lounge chair, and it works even better if you leave the house. Planes, trains, busses, ships, RVs and automobiles are the major methods of transportation. Other options are walking, hitchhiking, biking and motorcycling. Reading National Geographic magazine or being glued to the Travel or Discovery Channel doesn't count. You must make a physical voyage and not a transcendental spiritual journey to another geographical location. You must bring your body and all the baggage with you. Don't forget, wherever you go, there you are. Bring your toothbrush.

There's no doubt you have to travel to break into the world of fun. The reality treadmill you've been trapped on for years must come to a screeching and jolting halt. There are so many things to think about and plan for, besides a toothbrush, when you decide to bite the dust and travel someplace new. It's a daydream, and you may justify the reasons for re-entering the lounge chair world, but it's time to wake up. The moss is gathering on your north side. Follow the advice of *Canned Heat* in the 60's song, *On the Road Again*.

Travel in this definition does not mean to Auntie Ann's place ... unless she lives in Maui or Venice or the Grand Canyon (which would be a neat trick). Travel means vacation, to go on a journey, go from one place to another, a trip without extraterrestrial or chemically induced assistance.

Let's face it; preparing to travel is a harrowing experience and a definite deal buster right from the beginning. There's the ticket, the passport if you are going overseas, or even to Canada or Mexico, the ample supply of snacks and pills and pain killers, the right clothes (especially if you are leaving cold weather and heading for hot, or the reverse circumstances, heaven forbid), the amount of luggage you can carry, or fly with, or take on a bus, or haul to the taxi stand, or pack into your trunk, or carry into a motel by yourself in the middle of nowhere in the middle of the night.

Now what do you really want to take with you on a long vacation? Possibly it would be someone to carry your baggage to and from your chosen transportation, like maybe a butler or maid, or that other person who has been hanging around the house with you. And maybe the same person could iron your clothes when they are un-packed, un-wadded, and un-stuffed from your allowable baggage allotment.

The same person could massage your tired feet, back and overused brain cells. This person could carry a bell to warn you, alert you, when a milestone in your planned schedule is a looming doom. You know, when the train is leaving the station or the plane is about to land on the moon, or if you miss it, and you are in the middle of nowhere without a map.

In countless cases, and I'm sure there are many of you; a good bartender would be handy to have at hand and at your beckon call. A barkeep who knows the proper proportions of all the active ingredients that relax, tingle and at the same time stimulate the lagger muscle in your body that hasn't caught up with the jet-lag leg of the trip, namely, and most often, your brain.

Also, if possible, most would like to tow along that comfortable bed, entire bedroom, bathroom, kitchen and living room with the perfectly positioned lounge chair.

NOT!

But, let's not get ahead of ourselves. First a destination must be decided and etched in stone or scratched on the kitchen wall. Then a mode of transportation must be decided upon.

Going to Maui automatically eliminates train, bus and automobile. Going to Venice puts a damper on driving, at least on this side of the water. But going to Venice can be a wonderful combination of traveling modes. That is, fly to the East Coast (if you start anyplace else in the country (USA)), cruise on a ship to Europe, take a European train ride to Italy, rent a car and drive to Venice ... or anyplace else along the way, like the Romeo and Juliet Castle near Vicenza ... then take a waterbus along a centuries-old canal. There you have it, a multi-transportation schedule that was planned in hell; But what an experience you'll have.

And remember the truisms about the world's sub-divisions of national responsibilities when you travel: Home is where it seems the police are British, the chefs Italian, the mechanics German, the lovers French and it is all organized by the Swiss. But in a land unknown to you it is frequently, you will find, where the police are German, the chefs British, the mechanics French, the lovers Swiss, and it is all organized by the Italians.

Quote:

I travel not to go anywhere, but to go. I travel for travel's sake. The great affair is to move.

Robert Louis Stevenson

?

Seniors Have More Fun Because:

- Travel ranks among the top leisure activities for men and women over 50. They spend over $30 billion a year on vacation travel.
- Mature vacationers travel more frequently than any other age group, stay longer, and go further.
- They account for more than 72 % of all RV trips, 70 % of cruise passengers.
- Seniors spend 74 % more on a typical vacation than 18- to 49-year-olds.
- Seniors account for 80% of all luxury travel.
- Seniors account for 25% of all toy sales (Hmmm?).
- They buy 48% of luxury cars, 41% of all new cars and trucks.
- Seniors account for 77% of prescription drug sales and 61% of over-the counter drug sales.
- Seniors control $800 billion in discretionary income and account for fully half of all U.S. discretionary spending. Some 5 million seniors (14 %) are employed.
- Seniors have an income per capita that is 26% higher than the national average.
- Senior market is larger than African-American and Hispanic market segments combined.
- 30 million adults 50+ are now online, representing 37% of the 50+ population.
- Seniors spend more time online than teenagers.
- Seniors spend $10+ billion online annually.
- All this, yet seniors currently receive less than 10 % of all U.S. advertising messages.

Source: www.onmagazine.com

Traveling Seniors with Pets

Pets by Air

First of all, it is probably not a good idea if you want to have fun and are traveling overseas; unless of course it's your better half. Quarantine comes to mind, as well as international health certificates, traveling cages (temporary homes to the feint of heart), and changing planes (if you've lost your luggage while changing planes and became livid and fumed poisonous steam, can you imagine losing your pet to a flight to Paris when you are going to London? And worse, the pet may be having a better time than you). Finding hotels that accept pets can sometimes be a pain in the neck, and the same may be true of restaurants.

Pets by Car

If your pet has never been in a car, take it on short rides to get it ready for the trip. Schedule a check-up with your vet prior to your departure date, especially for animals with any long-term health concerns. Tranquilization (for the pet, not you) is usually not required for car trips, but if you know your pet gets carsick, consult your vet, and a light sedative (for the pet, not you) may be given.

Your pet should wear a collar with your name, address, and phone number at all times. Or, in case your pet can't read; have an ID microchip implanted just under the pet's skin near the scruff of the neck. This chip contains all of the information vital to returning the pet to you and the registration information is kept in databases available 24 hours a day. The version used in Europe even contains the pet's medical records and its favorite wine. If your pet strolls into a shelter or humane society and wants to check in, a scanner is run over it and identification is quickly made and your friend is safely returned to you.

Your pet should always be safely secured during the trip. Dogs should never be allowed to hang out of windows, even a window opened only slightly. Severe injuries can occur if you have to stop the car suddenly, and there's always the risk of the dog jumping out. A crate is recommended. It should be well ventilated, and be large enough for the pet to stand, turn around, and lie down. Line the bottom with a blanket to absorb urine in case of accident. Try not to travel in extreme weather conditions. If you must travel in hot weather, do so in early morning, or early evening.

NEVER leave your pet alone in a car, even for a few minutes. In hot weather, heat stroke can occur in minutes. In the Southwest outside temperatures reach the low 100s, but within minutes inside a car can climb to the 140s. The opposite it true in the North, Animals can freeze in cold temperatures. Also, it takes practically no time for someone to break into the car and take him.

Stop frequently (at least every hour and a half) to give your pet some food, water and exercise. DO NOT allow your dog or cat to run loose at rest areas. No matter how well trained an animal is, remember you are in a new place, and there are a lot of unusual noises. An accident can occur in seconds. When you arrive at your final stop, keep your pet in a quiet, calm area and give him lots of time to adjust to the new place.

Assorted other Pet Hints:

If you are flying with a penguin it is best to schedule an early morning flight when it is cool. Have an air-conditioned car waiting when you land, keep the hotel room and 50-60 degrees Fahrenheit and keep it that way all the time you are there, and bring plenty of ice.

Keep the birds in their cage and the fish in their bowl and snakes in a box, for obvious reasons.

Pets by Bike

Don't do it.

After all, if you've brought your pet, you probably want it to have fun, too ... not run all the way ... unless it can ride a bike.

Pets while Skiing

Same as Pets by Bike, but on skis, don't do it.

Staying In Top Form While Traveling

If you haven't detected, while you slurp your coffee as you sit staring out the kitchen window, most seniors are staying active. They care about their fitness and will work for it. It doesn't stop at home. It is also important to stay in shape on the road. For those 50 and older who fancy to spend their leisure time traveling, there are exercises that can be employed (excuse that word, please) by almost anyone – anywhere – anytime. All that is needed is room to stand, a few common items (a chair or a door knob, and don't get the wrong idea here), and the will to do it.

Some easy exercise tips to consider are:

Standing up straight ... a fine-tuned posture doesn't just look better; it helps blood flow through the body and the brain, a necessity so you won't forget who you are or where you are going. It also helps keep you from getting sore and stiffer than a shovel handle ... on long car and train rides or plane flights.

A stretch band is nice if you have one and remember to bring it. Resistance training is much easier with a stretch band, and it also allows you to do a greater variety of exercises and be able to modify the amount of resistance in a workout area about the size of an airline seat. One of the best benefits of using a stretch band for resistance training is that it can easily be customized to fit the situation. Simply by changing where the band is held, either the motel door handle or the back of a bar stool, the amount of resistance can be increased or decreased to suit your current fitness level and working space. Make sure the band is tight so you don't find yourself snapped into the back bar or into the restroom; that could hurt in more ways than one.

Knowing your limits is important while traveling; after all the nearest drugstore or aspirin may be 30,000 feet below. If you are having difficulty with any of the exercises, don't push it. For example, if traditional push ups are too challenging, try a wall push up instead, or leg squats using the back of the seat in front of you.

Of course, there are the obvious exercises while traveling. Squat ten times, with a suitcase in each hand, every time you have to move up one notch in the check-in line. Take long walks through the terminal, but that goes without saying. Stand up straight and rise and lower yourself on your toes, repeatedly. This flexes and tightens the leg muscles and feet. You may look pretty silly, but if anyone questions what you are doing, you can say, "Oh, I'm preparing to put my luggage in the overhead." Rise and lower your legs from a chair, or trip the other passengers who pass your seat in the waiting area. Or learn an advanced form of Terminal Chair or Airline Seat Kung Fu. I'm sure this will also entertain your fellow, bored passengers.

Watch what and how much you eat. It is easy to gorge yourself with food and gas when traveling because of the oftentimes boredom of layovers. It is true that travelers are often at the mercy of what is available, usually fast food, but there are still some steps anyone can take to eat healthy on the road. Fruits or sorbets if you can find them in a terminal, fat free dressing at the end of the salad bar, or order an appetizer as the main course. In some places this may mean French fries or onion rings.

Keeping a food and workout diary is an option, but generates little aerobic exercise. But it has a bonus, because this is also a good way to keep track of restaurants you like, or don't like, and want to visit, or not visit, on your next trip.

These tips should help you better manage your workouts and overall health while traveling. Following an exercise routine such as this one ... and remaining conscious about eating ... promotes an awareness of the body, and this is healthy at any age. So get packing, and don't forget the liniment.

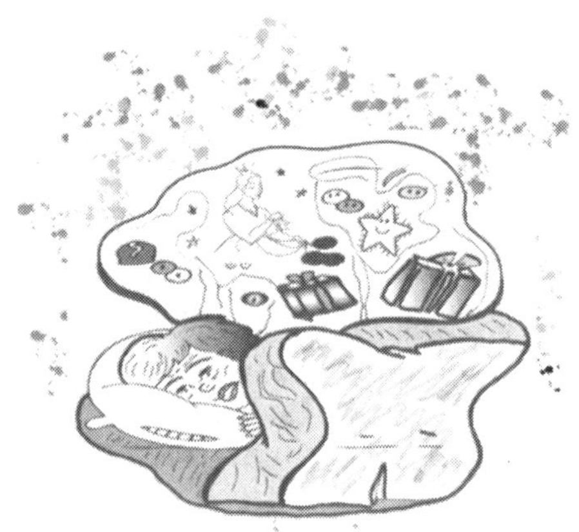

And Those Dreams, Fantasies, Loose Facts, Fiction, Jokes, and Elucidations

Information and events that come from semi-scientific papers, true stories told by a liar, the personal experiences as logged and blogged on the Internet and passed on as remedies and antidotes for the human condition, as well as just plain old made-up stuff. Whatever the origins, we apologize to anonymous; we had to print it without permission from whomever.

Many of these jokes and elucidations have been kicking around for years, then again, we only become a senior once in life and we have to play catch up.

What goes around comes around:

You float into a drugstore and tell the pharmacist you need some cyanide.

The pharmacist responds, "Why in the world do you need cyanide?"

You then explain that it is needed to poison your husband.

The pharmacist's eyes get big as Alka-Seltzer Tablets and he howls, "Lord have mercy, I can't give you a prescription for cyanide to kill your husband! That's against the law! They'll throw both of us in jail and I'll lose my license."

Then you reach into your purse and pull out a picture of your husband in bed with the pharmacist's wife, and hand it to him.

The pharmacist looks at the picture and replies, “Well now, you didn't tell me you had a prescription!”

This could be you

You walk into a jewelry store one Friday evening with a beautiful young gal at your side. You tell the jeweler you are looking for a special ring for your girlfriend. The jeweler looks through his stock and brings out a $5,000 ring and shows it to you.

You say, “I don't think you understand ... I want something very special.”

At that statement, the jeweler goes to his special stock and brings another ring over. “Here's a stunning ring at only $40,000” the jeweler says.

The young lady's eyes sparkle and her whole body trembles with excitement. You, seeing this say, “We'll take it.”

The jeweler asks how will the payment be made and you state by check. “I know you need to make sure the check is good,” you say, “so I'll write it now and you can call the bank on Monday to verify the funds and I'll pick the ring up Monday afternoon,”

Monday morning, a very teed-off jeweler phones you. "There’s no money in that account."

"I know", you say, "but can you imagine the weekend I just had?"

Senior men are just happier people

You could have been President, or maybe you are. You can never be pregnant. Same work, more pay, all your life. Wrinkles give you more character. People never stare at your chest when you're talking to them unless you are wearing an ‘*I’m With Stupid*’ T-Shirt.

The occasional perfectly designed belch is practically expected. New shoes don't maim you for life. Phone conversations last only 30 seconds unless you’re talking sports or broads. A five-day vacation requires only a single suitcase. You open most of your own jars and twist-off caps. You get extra credit for the slightest act of thoughtfulness. If someone forgets to invite you, he or she can still be your friend.

You almost never have strap problems in public. You are unable to see wrinkles in your clothes. Everything on your face stays its original color. The same hairstyle has lasted for years, maybe decades. You only have to shave your face and neck.

Your belly usually hides your big hips. One wallet and one pair of shoes one color for all seasons. You can wear shorts no matter how your legs look. You can DO your nails with a pocket knife. You have freedom of choice concerning growing a mustache, or not. You can do Christmas shopping for 25 relatives on December 24 in 25 minutes.

No wonder men are happier, but don't live as long.

Remember the days ...

You know the flight of your imagination: Things compared to how you were then, as to how you are now. If only things didn't change. You once had long hair, and now are longing for hair, and you moved to California because it was cool, and now live in Nevada because it's warm. You were going to hip joints instead of receiving a new hip joint, and listened to the Rolling Stones and not worrying about kidney stones.

In your youth you probably experienced acid rock and used stems and seeds, and today its consuming roughage and avoiding acid reflux. The local burger drive-in was in, now it's out. The hi-fi was at top volume but now the hearing aid is at top volume.

Your dreams were to look like Marlon Brando or Liz Taylor and drive a BMW, but now you don't want to look like either one of them and sometimes you are driven by your next BM. A KEG use to start your party-heart pumping and your feet dancing, now an EKG says 'stop drinking and dancing'.

An occasional trip to a Disco has been replaced by an occasional trip to Costco, that is, if you can pass the vision test instead of the driving test you once worried about. A trip to the principal's office has been replaced by calling the principal's office. You protested sending your peers into warfare, now you protest sending the same people into welfare.

But you can comfortably move on. You can't screw the system, but you can upgrade your system, or finally listen to your parents and get a haircut, or imitate your kids and shave your head:

Whatever ... Depends.

A Living Will to give up the Ghost for

This is the best living will around, it's easy to understand, and it makes perfect sense as well.

I, ______(your name here)______, being of sound mind and body, do not wish to be kept alive indefinitely by artificial means.

Under no circumstances should my fate be put in the hands of pinhead politicians who couldn't pass ninth-grade biology if their lives depended on it, or lawyers/doctors interested in simply running up the bills.

If a reasonable amount of time passes and I fail to ask for at least one of the following:

_______a Bloody Mary
_______a Margarita
_______a Martini
_______a Beer
_______a Rum and Coke
_______Steak and Baked Potato
_______Fried Chicken
_______the Remote Control
_______Chocolate
_______Sex

It should be presumed that I would not ever get better. When such a determination is reached, I hereby instruct my appointed person and attending physicians to pull the plug, reel in the tubes, and call it a day.

It's been a Helluva Run!

Signed________________________________

Date___________

The Middle of the Night

An 80-year-old man goes for a physical. All of his tests come back with normal results.

The doctor says, "Everything looks great. How are you doing mentally and emotionally? Are you at peace with God?"

He replies, "God and I are tight. He knows I have poor eyesight, so he's fixed it. So when I get up in the middle of the night to go to the bathroom, poof! The light goes on. When I'm done, poof! The light goes off."

"Wow, that's incredible," the doctor says.

A little later in the day, the doctor calls his wife.

The doctor says, "George is doing fine! But I had to call you because I'm in awe of his relationship with God. Is it true that he gets up during the night and poof! The light goes on in the bathroom, and when he's done, poof! The light goes off?"

"Oh my God!" his wife exclaims. "He's peeing in the refrigerator again!"

AAADD

Hooray!! They have finally found a diagnosis for my condition I had recently, (AAADD) Age Activated Attention Deficit Disorder.

This is how it goes: I decide to wash the car. I start toward the garage and I notice the mail on the table. OK, I'm going to wash the car, but first I'm going to go through the mail.

I lay the car keys down on the desk, discard the junk mail and I notice the trash can is full. OK, I'll just put the bills on my desk and take the trash can out. But since I'm going to be near the mailbox anyway, I'll pay these few bills first.

Now, where is my checkbook? Oops, there's only one check left. My extra checks are in my desk. Oh, there's the coke I was drinking. I'm going to look for those checks.

But first I need to put my coke further away from the computer. Oh, maybe I'll pop it into the fridge to keep it cold for a while.

I head toward the kitchen and my flowers catch my eye; they need some water. I set the coke on the counter and uh oh! There are my glasses. I was looking for them all morning! I'd better put them away first.

I fill a container with water and head for the flower pots -- Aaaaaagh! Someone left the TV remote in the kitchen. We'll never think to look in the kitchen tonight when we want to watch television so I'd better put it back in the family room where it belongs.

I splash some water into the pots and onto the floor, I throw the remote onto a soft cushion on the sofa and I head back down the hall trying to figure out what it was I was going to do?

End of Day:

The car isn't washed, the bills are unpaid, the coke is sitting on the kitchen counter, the flowers are half watered, the checkbook still only has one check in it and I can't seem to find my car keys! When I try to figure out how come nothing got done today, I'm baffled because I KNOW I WAS BUSY ALL DAY LONG!!!

I realize this is a serious condition and I'll get help, BUT FIRST I think I'll check my e-mail...

Religious Truths

Religious beliefs are an important part of having a fun-filled higher experience and you should know where you stand. Following are some much-abbreviated abstracts of the religions of the world and how they negatively affect your pursuit of fun. Read between the lines carefully, because one or more of these areas could apply to you, or all at once if you walk between a lot of lines or step on the cracks:

- **?** TAOISM -- S__t Happens
- **?** CONFUCIANISM -- Confucius say, " S__t happens"
- **?** ZEN BUDDISM -- What is the sound of S__t happening
- **?** HINDUISM -- This S__t happened before
- **?** ISLAM -- If S__t happens, it is the will of Allah
- **?** PROTESTANTISM -- Let S__t happen to someone else
- **?** CATHOLICISM -- If S__t happens, you deserve it
- **?** JUDAISM -- Why does S__t always happen to us
- **?** ATHEISM – S__t happens for no apparent reason
- **?** AGNOSTICISM -- We cannot prove that S__t happens
- **?** JEHOVAH'S WITNESS -- Let us in and we'll tell why S__t happens
- **?** CHRISTIAN SCIENCE -- Only good S__t happens
- **?** HARE KRISENA – S__t happens, S__t happens, happens, happens, S__t hap ...
- **?** EVANGELISM -- Send me $8,000,000 or S__t will happen to you
- **?** EXISTENTIALISM – S__t happens, and then we die

Pick your poison(s) carefully because your future beyond your current circumstances may depend upon it.

The Turtle in the Hat

While I was working in a bar in Seattle's Market, a longshoreman entered with a brown paper bag. He ordered a beer and peanuts. He started feeding the peanuts to whatever was in the bag. An elderly retired couple on vacation sat at the other end of the bar, obviously tourists, watching. Suddenly, the longshoreman jerked his hand back, picked up a pool cue and started beating the bag, yelling, 'that will teach you for biting me!' The couple asked what was in the bag, and the longshoreman replied that it was his pet turtle. The couple panicked and ran out the door. The longshoreman and a couple customers got a good laugh when he pulled his hardhat out of the bag.

The lesson here: Nothing is as it seems.

Retired Programmer

Did you hear about the Microsoft Windows programmer who died? He found himself in front of a committee that decides whether you go to Heaven or Hell.

The committee told the programmer he had some say in the matter and asked him if he wanted to see Heaven and Hell before stating his preference.

"Sure," he said, so an angel took him to a place with a sunny beach, volleyball, and rock and roll, where everyone was having a great time.

"Wow!" he exclaimed. "Heaven is great!"

"Wrong," said the angel. "That was Hell. Want to see Heaven?"

"Sure!" So the angel took him to another place. Here a bunch of people were sitting in a park playing bingo and feeding dead pigeons.

"This is Heaven?" asked the Windows programmer.

"Yup," said the angel.

"Then I'll take Hell." Instantly, he found himself plunged up to his neck in red-hot lava with the hosts of the damned in torment surrounding him. "Where's the beach? The music? The volleyball?" he screamed frantically to the angel.

"That was the demo," she replied as she vanished.

The New Priest

A new priest at his first mass was so nervous he could hardly speak. After mass he asked the elder and experienced monsignor how he had done. The monsignor replied, "When I am worried about getting nervous on the pulpit, I put a glass of vodka next to the water glass. If I start to get nervous I take a sip."

So the next Sunday he took the monsignor's advice. At the beginning of the sermon, he got nervous and took a drink. He proceeded to talk up a storm. Upon return to his office after mass he found the following note on his door:

1)	Sip the Vodka, don't gulp.
2)	There are 10 commandments, not 12.
3)	There are 12 disciples, not 10.
4)	Jesus was consecrated, not constipated.
5)	Jacob wagered his donkey, he did not bet his ass.
6)	We do not refer to Jesus Christ as the late J.C.
7)	The Father, Son, and Holy Ghost are not referred to as Daddy, Junior, and Spook.
8)	David slew Goliath; he did not kick the shit out of him.
9)	When David was hit by a rock and knocked off his donkey, don't say he was stoned off his ass.
10)	We do not refer to the cross as the Big T!
11)	When Jesus broke the bread at the Last Supper he said, "Take this and eat it, for it is my body", he did not say, "Eat me."
12)	The Virgin Mary is not referred to as the, "Mary with the Cherry".
13)	The recommended grace before a meal is not: "Rub-A-dub-dub, thanks for the grub, yeah God"
14)	Next Sunday there will be a taffy-pulling contest at St. Peter's, not a peter-pulling contest at St. Taffy's.
15)	And finally, the names of the four apostles are NOT Leonardo, Michelangelo, Donatello and Raphael.

The Biggest Scam

The Senate is investigating deceptive sweepstakes practices. These companies target the elderly and make them think they will receive a bunch of money, but in reality they never see any of it. The most deceptive and disparaging of these scams are called Social Security and Medicare.

When you're over 50...or so...

... Revealing and yet insignificant facts gathered over years of experience being a human and progressing toward the rank of senior first class. If you are a senior citizen:

- ? Kidnappers are not very interested in you.
- ? In a hostage situation you are likely to be released first.
- ? No one expects you to run into a burning building.
- ? People call at 9 p.m. and ask, "Did I wake you?"
- ? People no longer view you as a hypochondriac.
- ? There's nothing left to learn the hard way.
- ? Things you buy now won't wear out.
- ? You can eat dinner at 4 p.m.
- ? You can live without sex (but not without your glasses).
- ? You enjoy hearing about other people's operations.
- ? You get into a heated argument about pension plans.
- ? You have a party and the neighbors don't even realize it.
- ? You no longer think of speed limits as a challenge.
- ? You quit trying to hold your stomach in, no matter who walks into the room.
- ? You sing along with the elevator music.
- ? Your eyes won't get much worse.
- ? Your hearing won't get much worse.
- ? Your investment in health insurance is finally beginning to pay off.
- ? Your joints are more accurate meteorologists than the National Weather Service.
- ? Your secrets are safe with your friends because they can't remember them either.
- ? Your supply of brain cells is finally down to a manageable size.
- ? You can't remember who told you these facts.

Sex Advice for Seniors

- ☑ Put on your glasses ... on your eyes.
- ☑ Double check that your partner is actually in bed with you.
- ☑ Set timer for 10 minutes, in case you doze off in the middle.
- ☑ Set the mood with lighting. Turn them ALL OFF!
- ☑ Make sure you put 911 on your speed dial before you begin.
- ☑ Write partner's name on your hand in case you can't remember.
- ☑ Keep extra Polygrip close by so your teeth don't end up under the bed.
- ☑ Have Tylenol ready in case you actually complete the act.
- ☑ Make all the noise you want. The neighbors are deaf too.
- ☑ If it works, call everyone you know with the good news.
- ☑ Don't even think about trying it twice.

Stiff Neck

A man was walking down the street when he noticed that his grandfather was sitting on the porch, in the rocking chair, with nothing on from the waist down. “Grandpa, what are you doing?” the man exclaimed.

The old man looked off in the distance and did not answer his grandson. “Grandpa, what are you doing sitting out here with nothing on below the waist?” he asked again.

The old man slyly looked at him and said, “Well, last week I sat out here with no shirt on, and I got a stiff neck. This was your Grandma's idea!”

How Movies Changed

For the first time in many years, an elderly gentleman traveled from his rural town to the city to attend a movie. After buying his ticket, he stopped at the concession stand to purchase some popcorn. Handing the attendant $1.50, he couldn't help but comment, “The last time I came to the movies, popcorn was only 15 cents.”

"Well, sir," the attendant replied with a grin, "You're really going to enjoy yourself. We have sound now."

Retirees: The Whole Truth, Nothing but...

Question: How many days in a week?
Answer: 6 Saturdays, 1 Sunday

Question: When is a retiree's bedtime?
Answer: Three hours after he falls asleep on the couch.

Question: How many retirees to change a light bulb?
Answer: Only one, but it might take all day.

Question: What's the biggest gripe of retirees?
Answer: There is not enough time to get everything done.

Question: Why don't retirees mind being called seniors?
Answer: The term comes with a 10% discount.

Question: Among retirees what is considered formal attire?
Answer: Tied shoes.

Question: Why do retirees count pennies?
Answers: They are the only ones who have the time.

Question: What is the common term for someone who enjoys work and refuses to retire?
Answer: NUTS!

Question: Why are retirees so slow to clean out the basement, attic or garage?
Answer: They know that as soon as they do, one of their adult kids will want to store stuff there.

Question: What do retirees call a long lunch?
Answer: Normal.

Question: What is the best way to describe retirement?
Answers: The never ending Coffee Break.

Question: Why does a retiree often say he doesn't miss work, but misses the people he used to work with?
Answer: He is too polite to tell the whole truth.

Miscellaneous quotes and conversations

By: I don't know who said that, but ...

When an elderly woman was asked why she was standing in line to buy stamps from a teller when she could have used a stamp machine she replied: "The machine won't ask me about my arthritis!"

An old man in his eighties struggles to get up from the couch, and then starts putting on his coat.

His wife, seeing the unexpected behavior, asks: Where are you going?"

I'm going to the doctor, he replies.

Why, are you sick? His wife asks.

Nope. I'm going to get me some that Viagra stuff, he explains.

Immediately the wife starts working and positioning herself to get out of her rocker and begins to put on her coat.

Where the hell are you going, asks her husband?

I'm going to the doctor, too, she replies. If you're going to start using that rusty old thing, I'm getting a Tetanus shot.

Life should NOT be a journey to the grave with the intention of arriving safely in an attractive and well preserved body, but rather to >skid in sideways - Chardonnay in one hand - chocolate in the other -

>body thoroughly used up, totally worn out and screaming "WOO HOO, What a Ride

---

I've heard that cardiovascular exercise can prolong life; is this true?

Our heart is only good for so many beats, and that's it ... don't waste them on exercise. Everything wears out eventually. Speeding up your heart will not make you live longer; that's like saying you can extend the life of your car by driving it faster. Want to live longer? Take a nap.

Estate planning: Dan was a single guy living at home with his father and working in the family business. When he found out he was going to inherit a fortune when his sickly father died, he decided he needed a wife with which to share his fortune.

One evening at an investment meeting he spotted the most beautiful woman he had ever seen. Her natural beauty took his breath away.

'I may look like just an ordinary man,' he said to her, 'but in just a few years, my father will die, and I'll inherit 20 million dollars.' Impressed, the woman obtained his business card and three days later, she became his stepmother.

Moral: Women are so much better at estate planning than men.

? Who was Pancho?

Poetry

Monday Never Comes

Patrick M. Kennedy

After a long and crooked path,
it is a straight line from here to wherever.
The mornings are the afternoons
are the sleepless nights,
are the empty dreams.

On occasion a diversion passes by
then fades away like anticipation,
out of reach:
a small pause, a feint tick,
a failed campaign for action.

The days are the days are the days
are the hours rushing like minutes,
and like seconds, the next one never comes,
or too fast or too slow.
From here to there is non-stop.

One way, no doors, no days, no nights,
nowhere to go, no light.
Tuesday is Friday is Thursday is today,
every day is Sunday, the first of the week,
or maybe tomorrow, or maybe the last,

but Monday never comes.
It hides in a memory,
a shadow of history,
and a rhythm from the past.

Ode to Old Age

From: Retirement Jokes.com

There's quite an art to falling apart as the years go by,
And life doesn't begin at 40. That's a big fat lie.
My hair's getting thinner, my body is not;
The few teeth I have are beginning to rot.

I smell of Ben-Gay, not Chanel # 5;
My new pacemaker's all that keeps me alive.
When asked of my past, every detail I'll know,
But what was I doing 10 minutes ago?

Well, you get the idea, what more can I say?
I'm off to read the obituary, like I do every day;
If my names not there, I'll once again start -
Perfecting the art of falling apart

Ode to Cranky Men

Author Unknown

I chanced to pass a window
While walking through a mall
With nothing much upon my mind,
Quite blank as I recall. I noticed in that window
A cranky-faced old man,
And why he looked so cranky
I didn't understand. Just why he looked at ME that way
Was more than I could see
Until I came to realize
That cranky man was ME!

'Test for Fun' Questionnaire

In the past ...

You were last having fun when?	
You were last having fun where?	
You were having fun how?	
You were having fun with whom?	
You were having fun why?	
Your happiest moment was?	
Your sadist moment was?	
When did you bowl last?	
When did you go hiking last?	
... go biking last?	
... go dancing last?	
Have you ever cursed a golf ball?	
When did you stroll around the lake or along the river last?	
When did you last go window shopping?	
When did you last play softball, besides high school?	
When was the last time you went to a party or barbeque?	
... thrown a party or barbeque?	
... had a poker party?	

Have you joined an activity society like the Elks?	
... VFW?	
... Red Hat Society?	
When was the last time you went fishing?	
Are you satisfied where you are living?	
Do you like the weather where you are?	
Do you like the food where you are?	
Can you afford to live where you are?	
When was the last time you took a trip, other than to the market?	
What friends do you have the most fun with?	
Which or your friends would spoil your fun?	
When did you last go to a movie or a movie once a week?	
When did you last draw a picture?	
When did you last take a picture of something or someone you really liked?	
When was the last time you laughed out loud?	
When was the last time you smiled for no reason?	

Test Question Answers

1. *Who shot JR?*

Kristen Shepard (Mary Crosby) shot JR Ewing (Larry Hagman) in the Dallas TV series.

2. *You are about to enter another dimension, a dimension not only of sight and sound but of mind. A journey into a wondrous land of imagination. Next stop – WHERE?*

The Twilight Zone.

3. *What are Ricky's father, mother and brother's names?*

Ozzie and Harriet, and David Nelson

4. *What are Burma Shave Signs?*

Entertaining signs placed at intervals along the highways that were fun to read when traveling on roads across the United States.

A sample might go something like this:

When You're Frisky
From Whiskey
Don't Drive 'Cause
It's Risky
Burma Shave

Or:

The Poorest Guy
In The Human Race
Can Have
A Million-dollar Face
With
Burma Shave

5. *Who is Pvt. Gomer Pyle?*

The ever-genial comedian and silly singer, Jim Nabors.

6. *Who are Fibber McGee and Molly?*

Characters from a classic situation comedy radio program that aired from 1935 to 1959.

7. *Who are Amos and Andy?*

These were characters from one of the most popular radio shows in the 20th century. White actors played black actors, which created a little cloud over its aura, however, for 34 years from 1928 to 1956 Amos and Andy held an important place in the American old-time radio experience.

8. *Who is Red Ryder and who is Little Beaver?*

Red Ryder was newspaper comic western hero and a natural for the radio kids, from 1942 to 1952, with his Indian boy ward Little Beaver.

9. *What is the name of the princess on Howdy Doody Time?*

Princess, Summer Fall Winter Spring.

10. *What came into existence between 1946 and 1964?*

Probably you and millions of other Baby Boomers were rushed into the world after the wars.

11. *Who says "Wunnerful, Wunnerful, Wunnerful?" And who are his Sisters?*

Lawrence Welk and the singing Lennon Sisters.

12. *What costs about 23 cents per gallon?*

Gasoline in 1950.

13. *What is Highway Patrol, who starred in it, and what years was it active?*

A weekly TV program, starring Broderick Crawford – 1955 – 59.

14. *What year did the Edsel pass through the Golden Gates of misjudged marketing errors?*

1960

15. *Whose Father starred in the Sea Hunt?*

Actors Jeff and Beau Bridge's father was Lloyd, who played Mike Nelson, a frogman and underwater action hero.

16. *Who is Captain Kangaroo before he was Captain Kangaroo?*

Clarabelle the Clown on the Howdy Doody Show.

17. *"Rock Around the Clock"?*

A recording by Bill Haley & His Comets ... It is the first recording to be universally acknowledged as a rock and roll record. It is considered by many to be the song that put rock and roll on the map in America and around the world.

18. *Who said, "Plunk your magic twanger, Froggy!! ... And where?*

Froggy the Gremlin said it on the Buster Brown radio show.

19. *Buckwheat, Alfalfa, Spanky, Darla and Petey are members of what notorious gang, and when?*

Our Gang, or sometimes called, *The Little Rascals*, from the short-film kid's comedies of the 20's and 30's. I guess the names Buckwheat and Alfalfa made it too easy.

20. *A fiery horse with the speed of light, a cloud of dust and a hearty hi-yo Silver! ... Described who?*

It was the Lone Ranger with his faithful Indian companion Tonto ... Clayton Moore as the Lone Ranger and Jay Silverheels as Tonto.

21. *Who was Alben Barkley?*

He was the Vice-President of the United States with President Harry S. Truman. His popular nickname was "the Veep."

22. *What did Ray Kroc launch in 1955?*

McDonalds: Can you imagine people wanting a 15¢ burger (4¢ extra for cheese), a 5¢ coffee - and a third of them, a 20¢ milkshake! And all these people were being served at a speedy 15 seconds apiece. You know ... fast food! What do they cost now?

23. *In the 50's, Wham-O sold 25 million of these in two months?*

Hula-hoops.

24. Who was Pancho?

The Cisco Kid came to radio October 2, 1942, with Jackson Beck in the title role of The Cisco Kid and Louis Sorin as his as his sidekick Pancho.

The Author, Patrick M. Kennedy (Sir Pat)

Pat Kennedy has been a professional writer, editor, and graphic artist for over 30 years. In the past he has freelanced out of Seattle, Boise, Indianapolis, and Las Vegas.

He has published a novel, *Toy Shadows*, and has had articles published in various magazines and books. He is especially proud that he still writes a regular humorous and lighthearted column, '*Inside Out & Round About*' that is available and distributed through the *Senior Wire News Service*, and contributes a regular senior's column to the *Upriver Community News*. These articles are the foundation of this book.

Over time, he has worked as a paperboy, professional musician, elevator operator, shipping clerk, soldier, teletype operator, bartender, bar owner, janitor, advertising agency owner, editor for several small literary publications, publisher, copywriter, art gallery owner, custom picture framer, salesman, and for the last few years as a technical writer for Fortune 500 companies. This gives him a wide-ranging list of experience to call on for his writing and editing."

Lightning Source UK Ltd.
Milton Keynes UK
UKOW021256201211

184119UK00011B/97/P